Mountain Biking
Jackson Hole

AMBER TRAVSKY

D0829935

FALCON®

Guilford, Connecticut

An imprint of The Globe Pequot Press

This book is dedicated to Rich,
for his encouragement and support,
and to my mom and dad for teaching me respect and love for
the outdoors at an early age. All those camping trips and
Sunday picnics made a lasting impression.

A FALCON GUIDE ®

Copyright © 2001 by The Globe Pequot Press

Cover photo: Cheyenne Rouse Photography

Library of Congress Cataloging-in-Publication Data
Travsky, Amber, 1955–
    Mountain biking Jackson Hole / Amber Travsky.— 1st ed.
        p. cm. — (A Falcon guide)
    ISBN 1-56044-749-4
    1. All terrain cycling—Wyoming—Jackson Hole Region—Guidebooks. 2. Jackson Hole Region (Wyo.)—Guidebooks. I. Title. II. Series.

GV1045.5.W82 J338 2001
796.6'3'0978755—dc21

                                                              2001023644

Manufactured in the United States of America
First Edition/First Printing

 Printed on recycled paper.

Contents

Acknowledgments

Exploring the backcountry for this book was a labor of love. Darth the wonder dog, my Australian shepherd, was my constant companion. Rich, my husband for these past 18 years, wasn't with me on the trail but he provided encouragement and support from my home base in Laramie. I thank him for all he has done to help me in my endeavors.

I am a Wyoming native and have been blessed with the opportunity to explore the little nooks and crannies of this state. One of the outstanding qualities of this state is the people who are willing to lend a hand and spare a kind word. Thanks to all you un-named well-wishers. Many, many thanks to the hikers and bikers who offered friendly words and helpful advice on the trails. I enjoyed my solitude but also relished meeting other outdoor enthusiasts on the trail.

Thanks to Fred Torrence at Adventure Sports/Dornan's in Moose. Not only did he help me with bike repairs but he also shared information on bike routes and trail recommendations.

The staff at the Bridger-Teton National Forest, including Linda Merigliano, provided route recommendations and answered my questions on route selection.

And, last but not least, thanks to Peggy O'Neill-McLeod at Falcon Publishing for offering me this project and the chance to explore Wyoming's northwest corner.

MAP LEGEND

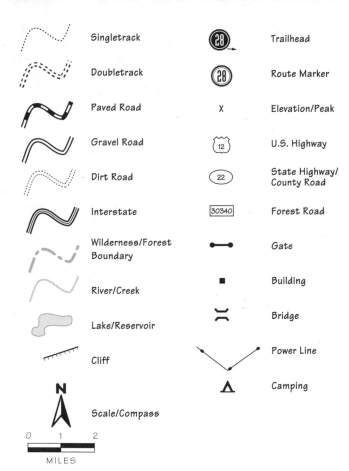

Singletrack

Doubletrack

Paved Road

Gravel Road

Dirt Road

Interstate

Wilderness/Forest Boundary

River/Creek

Lake/Reservoir

Cliff

Scale/Compass

Trailhead

Route Marker

Elevation/Peak

U.S. Highway

State Highway/ County Road

Forest Road

Gate

Building

Bridge

Power Line

Camping

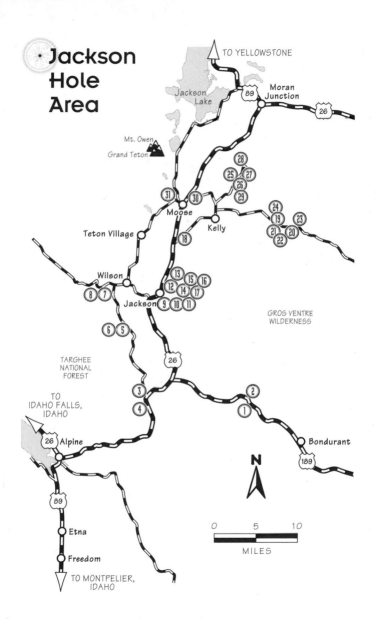

Get Ready to CRANK!

It's a tough assignment to spend weeks mountain biking in the shadow of the Teton Mountains. Those jagged peaks were just over my shoulder during most of the rides in this book.

The Jackson Hole area is truly one of our nation's jewels and it offers excellent biking for the fat-tire enthusiast. The town of Jackson is busy and crowded and I expected the trails to be the same. I was pleasantly surprised to discover I could find solitude within 15 minutes of Jackson in nearly any direction.

Compared to many Wyoming communities, Jackson traffic is hectic and it moves at a frenzied pace. Crowds and traffic extend into the adjacent Grand Teton and Yellowstone National Parks. But, if you go even a short distance off the beaten track, the crowds disappear.

In one 10-day period in late August, I met only a half dozen cyclists, four hikers, two ATV riders, and two guys on motorcycles on the trails.

Campgrounds in the national parks are typically full throughout the summer. But that's not true for those campgrounds or dispersed camping areas on national forest lands. There's plenty of space for those wanting a little elbow room.

The rides in this book offer a sampling of the many roads and trails available for mountain biking around Jackson Hole. Biking in Grand Teton National Park is limited to existing roads and a few trails but there are miles and miles of trails in nearby national forests. Respect wilderness area boundaries. There is plenty of non-wilderness backcountry to keep a cyclist pedaling for many seasons.

How to Use This Guide

Mountain Biking Jackson Hole provides descriptions and directions for a wide range of rides, from difficult crankers to family cruises. When you select rides in this book, it is easy to match up your technical and fitness levels with an appropriate ride. Most of the rides are either loops or out-and-back routes, although there are also a few shuttle rides that involve drop-off and pick-up points.

Each ride has been described in one direction. Reversing the route may completely alter the difficulty and make the route seem completely different.

Rides follow a combination of road and trail surfaces. Portions of some rides follow gravel and even paved roads, allowing cyclists to enjoy the scenery and not worry so much about the technical aspects of mountain biking. Others follow doubletrack roads. This is a general descriptor for roads that have two parallel paths, typically for four-wheel-drive vehicle use. The condition of doubletrack varies widely, from rough and rocky to smooth and flat.

The increased use of all-terrain vehicles, or ATVs, has added a new type of road. These are narrower than typical doubletrack, with a wide singletrack, and are generally excellent for mountain biking. Other routes follow singletrack paths that are also used by hikers and horseback riders.

The rides in this book are described using the headings and definitions listed below:

Trail name and number: Each ride is given a name and number. Names are based on topographic or other features in the area, official names assigned by land managers, or local custom. Numbers are provided to allow easy reference when one ride can easily be linked with another.

Location: This description provides the general location based on nearby towns or landmarks.

Distance: The overall length of a trail is described in miles. Also, the trail is usually described either as a loop, one-way, or out-and-back route.

Time: A rough estimate of the time needed to complete the ride is provided. This includes actual riding time and does not include rest stops. Strong, skilled cyclists may be able to complete the ride in less time than listed, while others may take considerably longer. Also, trail conditions, weather changes, and mechanical problems can greatly influence the duration of a ride.

Tread: This describes the type of road or trail, including paved road, gravel road, dirt road, doubletrack, ATV-width singletrack, and singletrack. Often the distinction between the tread types is not always obvious. For example, a doubletrack road, closed to motorized travel, may gradually become a singletrack. Also, gravel roads and dirt roads can be difficult to differentiate.

Season: This is the best time of year to pedal the route, taking into account variations in precipitation from year to year and trail conditions.

Aerobic level: This describes the physical effort required to complete the ride in general terms: easy, moderate, or strenuous. An explanation of this rating system is included later in this chapter.

Technical difficulty: This describes the level of bike handling skills needed to complete the ride. A thorough description of the rating scale is described later in this chapter.

Hazards: Potential dangers or other hazards are listed. These include traffic, weather, trail obstacles and conditions, risky stream crossings, difficult route finding, and other potential perils. It is important to keep in mind that trail conditions can change with time. New fences can be constructed and additional routes may have been added since these routes were originally researched.

Highlights: This section details the qualities that make the ride unique. You'll find specifics on things you'll see along the way and a general description of natural surroundings.

Land status: The land ownership and the federal agency managing the land will be listed. All of the rides in this book are on public lands, except for occasional public-access roads where the federal managing agency has secured right-of-way access across private land. When a route crosses private land it will be noted and special care must be taken to remain on the access road until it enters public land.

Maps: U.S. Geological Survey (USGS) topographic maps that cover a ride will be listed along with any special-use maps that are available.

Access: A description is provided of how to get to the trail-head or starting point of the ride.

The ride: A detailed description is provided, listing key points such as landmarks, notable climbs and descents, stream crossings, obstacles, hazards, major turns, and junctions. All distances are measured to the tenth of a mile with a cycle-odometer. Terrain, riding technique, and even tire pressure can affect odometer readings; treat all mileages as estimates.

Elevation profiles: Each ride is illustrated with a graph that includes elevation changes, tread types, and technical ratings. The elevation profile illustrates changes in altitude. This can help in selecting a ride that meets your needs and it helps prepare you for what terrain changes are coming as the ride progresses.

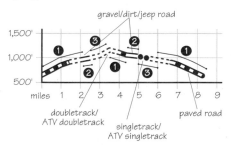

The Ratings

I have had friends confide in me their anxiety about an up-coming ride with another friend. "Is this a hard trail?" they ask. Their anxiety arises from concern that what their friend considers an easy ride, will, in reality, be a leg-burning, arm-jarring experience. All they really want is a pleasant and smooth ride through the woods.

Such anxiety is not without merit. One person's easy ride can be a heart-pounding experience for the novice rider. How can you know in advance what the trail is really like? Don't listen to your friends. Read this book instead.

Each ride has two ratings: a technical rating and an aerobic rating. The technical rating provides an indication of the bike skills needed to successfully negotiate a trail. The aerobic scale indicates what your heart rate will be as you pedal the ride. The following sections define the various ratings.

Technical Difficulty Ratings

The technical ratings in this book go from a low of 1—the smooth, paved road, to 5—the gnarly hair-raiser. The ratings are based on an objective approach based on such things as the width of the trail and the frequency of obstacles such as rocks and ruts. The addition of a plus (+) symbol helps cover gray areas between levels of difficulty. A rating of 3+ is slightly more technically difficult than a rating of 3. A description for each of the five ratings is provided below.

Level 1: Smooth tread. It is most likely a paved road or has smooth, even gravel. There are no obstacles or ruts. This requires only basic bike riding skills.

Level 2: Mostly smooth tread. This is most likely an improved road, though occasional obstacles, such as ruts and rocks, are present. It may also be a doubletrack or an ATV trail in good condition.

Level 3: Irregular tread with some rough sections. This includes rougher doubletrack where ruts, rock, loose gravel, or sand create obstacles. It also includes singletrack and ATV trails with occasional rocky areas where the less-experienced rider may need to get off the bike and hike around unsafe areas.

Level 4: This is similar to Level 3, except the obstacles are much more frequent. The rocky sections combine with steep terrain and the rider must focus on the road ahead: no daydreaming! Bike-hiking becomes more frequent for the less-experienced rider.

Level 5: This is a continuously broken, rocky, and root-infested trail. Most often it is a singletrack trail, but it can also be a doubletrack road. There are frequent and sudden changes in gradient, with some very steep areas going over rocky terrain. The obstacles are nearly continuous. Only the most experienced—or totally insane—cyclist will stay on the bike in these conditions. Bike-hiking, even carrying the bike, is the typical mode of transport on these sections.

Aerobic Levels

The effort involved in pedaling a bicycle varies considerably among individuals as fitness levels vary. Terrain, elevation changes, and duration of a ride can greatly influence the aerobic level of a ride. As the heart rate and breathing rate increase and sweat breaks out, the aerobic level goes up. The physical exertion ratings, from easy to strenuous, are defined below.

Easy: The heart rate is well below maximum and, although the breathing rate may be slightly elevated, it is well within levels that can be maintained over a sustained period.

Typically, the ride is going downhill. The easy level may also include rides through rolling terrain with short but gradual climbs. You will get a light workout at this level and a little sweat may break out on your brow.

Moderate: This level will provide a moderate to good workout depending on the duration of the ride. There are some hills and although the climbs are fairly short, they may be fairly steep. The heart rate is still within the aerobic training zone, or 70 to 85 percent below the maximum.

Strenuous: This level may require occasional rest periods. At this level the heart rate can approach maximum. On some of these rides the climbs still level out enough to provide some easing of the heart rate. Other rides can be very strenuous, or "killer," with terrain mostly uphill and quite steep. To continue riding at the very strenuous level requires a high level of aerobic fitness, power, and endurance. Mere mortals will need to walk.

The Journey

The Jackson Hole Area:
What to Expect

Jackson is surrounded by national forest and national park lands. This provides considerable opportunity for mountain biking through some of the most spectacular scenery on the planet. Cycling in both Grand Teton and Yellowstone National Parks is limited to existing roads, although a few gravel roads have been closed to motorized travel and are ideal for mountain biking. Mountain bikes are not allowed on the park's hiking trails.

The Gros Ventre Wilderness Area, Teton Wilderness Area, and Jedediah Smith Wilderness Area are all off-limits to mountain bikes but plenty of non-wilderness remains to be explored.

This is grizzly and black bear country; care must be taken to ensure safety. Read the introduction of this book for some general directions and check with Park and Forest Rangers for additional information.

Snow comes to this part of the state early in the fall and stays well into spring and even summer at the higher elevations. To prevent damage to trails, be sure to wait until the routes are clear of snow and are mostly dry before venturing out. Also, take along some bug repellent if you plan to stop for a picnic. One of the best times of year to bike this area is late August and into September when many of the bugs are gone. Take care if you bike during the hunting season, though, and wear plenty of hunter orange clothing. This is a very popular hunting area.

Weather

The fundamental rule in Wyoming is to be prepared for anything. Natives jokingly remind visitors if they don't like the weather, just wait. It will change in five minutes. A sunny blue sky can give way to a hailstorm in a half-hour. Snow has been reported in the high country every month of the year. Be prepared.

For those not accustomed to Wyoming weather, the seasonal changes can provide the greatest surprises. Actually, it's not the changes, but their timing. Residents joke, "There are two seasons in Wyoming—winter, and the Fourth of July."

Mountain biking in Wyoming is possible throughout the year for those willing to wear extra clothing and brave the wind and cold. Hard-core riders equip their bikes with studded tires or tire chains. The majority of mountain bikers begin their pedaling season in the spring, pedaling the lower elevations until snow leaves the high country. Often, snowdrifts linger at elevations above 9,500 feet until early July.

Spring can be especially unpredictable, with calm winds and warm temperatures one day, changing to cold sleet and snow the next. As temperatures rise, frozen roads thaw and turn into paths of mud and gumbo.

Summer is especially pleasant in the mountains, where temperatures rarely exceed the 80s during the day, while dropping to the 40s and 50s at night.

Fall has the most predictable weather, as Indian

summer extends into September and October with crisp mornings, mild daytime temperatures, and chilly evenings. This is a great time to be in the woods, but take extra precautions during the hunting season. Wear a hunter orange vest and avoid biking into areas when you hear shooting.

Blue skies are common in Wyoming. But the low humidity and high intensity of the sun require special precautions.

Keep well hydrated. The low humidity may keep you from visibly sweating, but that doesn't mean you aren't losing water. Don't wait until you're thirsty to start drinking; your sense of thirst lags behind your real need for water. Fully hydrate before and after the ride. When on the bike, drink at least every 15 minutes and at least a pint an hour, even if you don't feel thirsty. The use of a water bladder is a smart alternative where you can regularly sip water instead of having to reach for a water bottle.

Wyoming's high altitude makes the sun more intense. Use a sunscreen. Wear a shirt that is light colored, lightweight, and has long sleeves that you can roll down or up.

Clothing Considerations

As mentioned, Wyoming weather can be unpredictable. Many of the rides in this book are in the backcountry, where little assistance can be expected if you need help. Go prepared.

The smartest approach to clothing is to wear layers. Many special fabrics are available that wick moisture away from the skin. Polypropylene or similar material should be worn next to the skin. Stay away from cotton; as you sweat it will absorb water and hold it. When you stop and the temperatures are cool, wet fabric next to the skin can create a dangerous chilling effect.

When going to the high country it is important to remember there can be a drop in temperature of up to 10 degrees F for every 1,000-foot gain in elevation. Typically, if it is 90 degrees F on the prairie at 5,000 feet, temperatures will be in the 60s and 70s at 8,000 to 10,000 feet and even lower at higher elevations or if the wind is blowing.

Carry an extra long-sleeved shirt and a rain jacket even in the middle of August. Some cyclists prefer to carry leg and arm warmers, which are sleeve-like pieces of clothing that you can slide on and off with changes in temperature. Full-fingered gloves, a hat or balaclava that fits under a helmet, and an extra pair of socks are also good additions for spring, early summer, and fall riding.

Exploring the Backcountry

There are some "rules of the backcountry" that dictate both courtesy and responsibility.

Fences: There is a cardinal rule in Wyoming concerning gates: when you pass through a gate leave it the way you found it. In other words, if the gate was closed, reclose it. If it was open, keep it open. Some barbed wire fences can be especially tricky to open and close. The best technique is to put your shoulder against the gate, reach through the fence for the post, and pull it in, using your entire body if necessary. Most gates have a metal staple attached and the gate wire needs to go under this staple to prevent cattle from being able to lift the wire when they rub against the gate. If you come across a locked gate when you are sure you are on a public access road, be sure to report it to the land manager. It is possible that access is being illegally restricted.

Water: It is wise to be prepared to refill water bottles from available natural water sources. Though you may think you are carrying enough water at the start of a ride, it is not unusual to run out. Leaning over and drinking from a cool, clear, mountain stream may sound romantic and look good in the movies, but it is not a safe move. Even clear, clean water at high elevations can carry nasty organisms that wreak havoc with the human intestinal tract.

There are a number of commercially produced water filters on the market and the selection of a specific brand and model is a personal preference. As the cost of a filter increases, usually its ability to filter also increases. Less expensive models may not filter out Giardia, so check the product description carefully.

The other option for water purification, aside from boiling water, is to use iodine tablets. Most tablets today are accompanied by a second tablet that will remove the iodine, and thus the iodine taste, from the water once it is purified. I have used the iodine method for years. It is hard to beat the weight and cost. However, if you are getting water with a high sediment content the iodine does nothing to filter out the particles.

Mosquitoes and other annoying pests: Mosquito Lake and Mosquito Creek are frequent monikers in the high country. Although I haven't encountered a Black Fly Lake, No-See-'Em Pond, or Horsefly Creek, these names would be equally descriptive of many places in Wyoming, both in the high country and on the prairie. Mosquitoes and other flying pests are especially numerous in the high country during July and early August. Take along some bug repellent.

Biking in bear country: A couple of precautions should be taken when in bear country. While cycling, keep alert to bear signs and change your direction if necessary. Making some noise when you bike in areas with dense brush can help alert a bear to your presence. Noise gives the bear notice that you are present; often, violent responses from bears are a result of the bear being surprised. Making noise can prevent this type of response.

If you camp in bear country, do not have food stored or prepared near your tent. In Yellowstone and Grand Teton National Parks large metal bear-proof boxes are provided in the campsites. Store your gear and all food in these boxes. If there is no bear box, store food well away from your sleeping area and sling it high up in a tree.

Pepper sprays are a popular weapon to deter an advancing bear. Some evidence indicates bears may be attracted to pepper spray, but the experts still recommend using a top-strength pepper spray.

Encountering other wildlife: Wyoming is rich with wildlife. Keep your eyes open; you never know what you might see. From big game species, such as elk, moose, mule deer, and pronghorn, to smaller mammals, including pine martens, marmots, and porcupines, the opportunity for wildlife viewing is excellent. Give all wildlife a wide berth both for safety reasons and to ensure the health of the animal.

Tips to Keep Yourself Found

Compass: It is important to keep track of the direction you are headed and the direction you want to go. Relying on the position of the sun is fine to some extent, but clouds can obscure it and you may not realize you are changing direction or going the wrong way until it is too late. I carry a compass at all times and even have one attached to my bike.

Maps: The maps in this book, when used in conjunction with the route directions, will, in most instances, be sufficient to get you to the trail and keep you on it. However, the maps cannot begin to provide the detailed information found in U.S. Geological Survey 7.5-minute topographic maps (usually at a scale of 1 to 24,000). These "topo" maps are especially useful for determining terrain. The maps have contour lines that are typically spaced to represent a specific change in elevation. An explanation on the legend of the map will define the contour interval—the change in elevation represented between two contour lines; most often, the distance is 40 feet. When the contour lines are closer together, they indicate that the slope is steeper.

Maps printed by land management agencies, such as the Bureau of Land Management (BLM) and the U.S. Forest Service are in a scale of 1 to 100,000. These maps are especially useful in getting the big picture of an area, but they may not always show contour lines.

Helpful hints: Having spent considerable time in the backcountry, there have been times when I was temporarily "misplaced." If this happens to you, don't panic. To help determine your location, here are a few tips:

1. Fences tend to be on section lines. This is not always true, but, in general, fences tend to go along section lines (a section is a 1-mile square designation on a map) or, at least, on half or quarter section lines.

2. All oil and gas pump sites have signs giving their legal description. If you misplace yourself in oil and gas developed areas, it is handy to verify your location by looking at the legal description sign posted at every drill site. Of course, this only helps if you have a map that includes township, range, and section delineations.

3. Look back from time to time. As you ride along, and especially if you are going cross-country, occasionally look back in the direction you have come. Things can look different from the other direction and it can be helpful, if you have to retrace your route, to pinpoint landmarks from a different perspective.

4. Many trails on public lands have blaze marks. These marks, a dot-dash placed one above the other, are especially useful if snow obscures some of the trail. Most blazes are about 7 to 9 feet up on trees and the first mark, or dot, is circular with a diameter of about 4 inches. The second mark, or dash, is right below and is an oblong cut in the tree about 8 to 10 inches long and 4 inches wide. Some dot-dashes are highlighted with bright orange or red paint.

5. Trails are often marked with rock cairns when they go across treeless terrain. These cairns range in size from a pile of three or four rocks, to elaborate affairs with a couple dozen rocks arranged in a pyramid fashion. These are especially useful when crossing rock fields or grassy meadows, where a trail is easily obscured.

6. If you lose the trail, relocate it using a systematic process. Rather than wandering forward for an extended period, once you lose a trail, stop and systematically try to relocate it. When this happens to me, I set my bike down at the end of the known trail and then scout the area in a fan-like pattern, searching for dot-dashes on the trees or looking for obvious foot trails. Trails can easily be lost when you enter large meadows or sagebrush openings. In heavily grazed areas cattle can create significant trails. These may look like notable, well-established routes one minute and then suddenly dissipate into nothing or dead-end at a waterhole or salt lick. The same can be true of game trails. If you are not familiar with route finding, proceed cautiously. Infrequently used trails can be difficult to locate.

All of the trails in this book were well marked and easy to follow at the time of the initial mapping. But conditions can change with time. Carry a map and compass at all times and don't wander aimlessly if you lose a trail; relax and search in a systematic manner.

IMBA Rules of the Trail

The majority of routes in this book are on multi-use roads and trails. To avoid conflicts with other users, some rules of the trail need to be followed. Do your part to maintain trail access by observing the following rules of the trail formulated by the International Mountain Bicycling Association (IMBA). IMBA's mission is to promote environmentally sound and socially responsible mountain biking.

1. Ride on open trails only. Respect trail and road closures, avoid possible trespass on private land, and obtain permits and authorization as may be required. Federal and state wilderness areas are closed to cycling. The way you ride will influence trail management decisions and policies.

2. Leave no trace. Be sensitive to the dirt beneath you. Even on open (legal) trails, you should not ride under conditions where you will leave evidence of your passing, such as on certain soils after a rain. Recognize different types of soil and trail construction; practice low-impact cycling. This also means staying on existing trails and not creating any new ones. Be sure to pack out at least as much as you pack in.

3. Control your bicycle! Inattention for even a second can cause problems. Obey all bicycle speed regulations and recommendations.

4. Always yield the trail. Make known your approach well in advance. A friendly greeting is considerate and works well; don't startle others. Show your respect when passing by slowing to a walking pace or even stopping. Anticipate other trail users around corners or in blind spots.

5. Never spook animals. An unannounced approach, a sudden movement, or a loud noise startles all animals. This can be dangerous for you, others, and the animals. Give animals extra room and time to adjust to you. When passing horses use special care and follow directions from the horseback riders (ask them if you're uncertain). Running cattle and disturbing wildlife is a serious offense. Leave gates as you find them or as marked.

6. Plan ahead. Know your equipment, your ability, and the area in which you are riding, and prepare accordingly. Be self-sufficient at all times, keep your equipment in good repair, and carry necessary supplies for changes in weather or other conditions. A well-executed trip is a satisfaction to you and not a burden or offense to others. Always wear a helmet.

Getting Ready to Ride

You've selected your route and are getting set to head out. To ensure a safe and fun outing, you should carry the following items, either in a small pack on the bike or in a day/fanny pack. This list is not meant to be all-inclusive, but rather includes minimum health and safety items. Longer rides or overnighters will require additional equipment and supplies.

There are several bicycle tools on the market that combine a number of different tools into a small, handy gadget. This equipment list includes individual tools, but these combination gadgets can be substituted.

This book
Additional maps
Compass
Tire levers
Bike pump
Patch kit
Spare tube
Allen wrenches (3, 4, 5, and 6 mm)
6-inch crescent wrench
Small flat-blade screwdriver
Chain rivet tool
Spoke wrench
Baling wire

Duct tape
First-aid kit (sunscreen, aspirin, various bandages and gauze, moleskin, etc.)
Water purification tablets or filter
Extra long-sleeved shirt
Wind jacket
Leggings
Food
Water
More water

Hoback Canyon

The Hoback River got its name in 1811 from John Hoback, a trapper and guide. Towering cliffs tower over the river along US Highway 189-191. Breaks in the canyon provide access to the backcountry but the close proximity to the Gros Ventre Wilderness Area on the north side of the canyon limits biking in that direction. The Wyoming Range can be accessed from the south side of the canyon. The Wyoming Range is probably the least known of all Wyoming's mountain ranges. It's a great place to bike for the adventurer seeking solitude.

Cliff Creek Falls

Location: The Wyoming Range, south of the Hoback River.

Distance: 12.8 miles, out and back.

Time: 4 to 5 hours.

Tread: Singletrack.

Season: From late spring into fall.

Aerobic level: Moderate.

Technical difficulty: 4

Hazards: Rocks, logs, waterbars, and other obstacles on and next to the trail.

Highlights: Sudden twists and turns to avoid obstacles; this is one of the most fun and challenging singletrack routes in this book.

Land status: Bridger-Teton National Forest.

Maps: USGS Triple Peak, Lookout Mountain.

Access: Six miles west of Bondurant, exit from U.S. Highway 189-191 (Hoback Canyon Road) at Forest Road 30530. Continue south on gravel road for 7 miles to the end of the road and trailhead. There is camping and parking available at the trailhead.

Option: From the falls, the trail continues another 2 miles to Cliff Creek Pass.

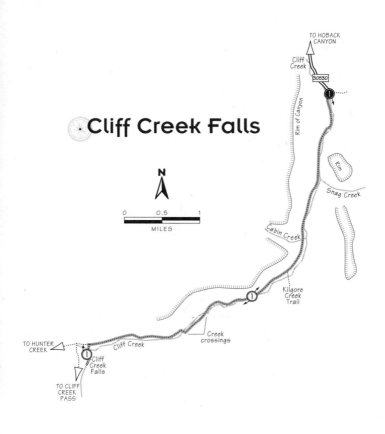

Cliff Creek Falls

TO HOBACK
CANYON

Cliff
Creek

30530

Rim of Canyon

Rim

Snag Creek

Cabin Creek

Kilgore
Creek
Trail

N

0   0.5   1
MILES

Creek
crossings

TO HUNTER
CREEK

Cliff Creek

Cliff
Creek
Falls

TO CLIFF
CREEK
PASS

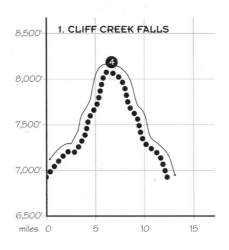

1. CLIFF CREEK FALLS

The ride

0.0	From trailhead, cross bridge to start of route.
2.3	Cross small creek.
2.7	Trail forks. Go right. Kilgore Creek Trail goes left.
3.8	Cross small creek.
4.2	Cross Cliff Creek. This is a wet crossing and requires wading across the creek.
4.8	Cross back across Cliff Creek.
4.9	Cross little creek (it may not be flowing).
5.2	Cross little creek.
5.3	Cross little creek (only 18 inches across).
5.4	Skirt around a little pond.
5.6	Cross little creek and canyon opens up. Vegetation is dense and may hide the trail.
6.3	Cross creek to the falls.
6.4	At the falls. Turnaround point. Return on same route.
12.8	Back at starting point.

Granite Creek

Location: The Gros Ventre Mountains, north of the Hoback River.

Distance: 18.9-mile loop.

Time: Two to three hours.

Tread: Gravel road and singletrack.

Season: From late spring into fall.

Aerobic level: Moderate.

Technical difficulty: 2 on gravel road, 3 to 4 on singletrack.

Hazards: Traffic; washboarded road; steep sections of singletrack that are safer to bike hike than to ride.

Highlights: Paralleling Granite Creek; cliffs along the trail; Granite Hot Springs.

Land status: Bridger-Teton National Forest.

Maps: USGS Bull Creek, Granite Falls.

Access: Approximately 11 miles east of Hoback Junction on U.S. Highway 189-191, exit just before the bridge crossing of the Hoback River, onto Forest Road 30530 leading to Granite Recreation Area. Go 0.1 mile up the road and park in wide gravel area near the creek.

Option: For a short and fun 3.5-mile loop, begin at Granite Creek Campground, going up road to hot springs, crossing to singletrack, and looping back below the campground before returning to the starting point.

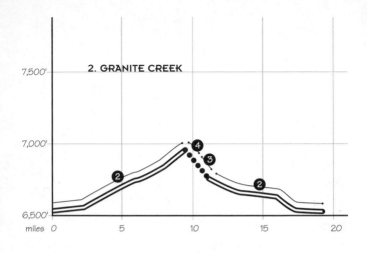

7,500'

2. GRANITE CREEK

7,000'

6,500'

miles 0   5   10   15   20

The ride

0.0 Head up main gravel road, going toward the hot springs.

0.3 Pass by a couple of portable outhouses. (They may be moved in the future but are there primarily for use during the snowmobile season.)

1.3 Road forks. Go right and over bridge.

3.7 Start steeper climb.

4.0 At top of tough hill.

4.7 Doubletrack goes right. Stay on main road.

6.7 Road forks. Stay straight. Right is FR 30519.

7.7 Footpaths go left and a gravel road forks right. Stay straight on main road.

8.5 Pass by Granite Creek Campground.

8.7 Road forks. Right goes to Granite Falls. Stay straight.

9.2 At end of main road. Continue straight.

9.3 Cross footbridge and go right onto singletrack to begin fun, and sometimes challenging, downhill.

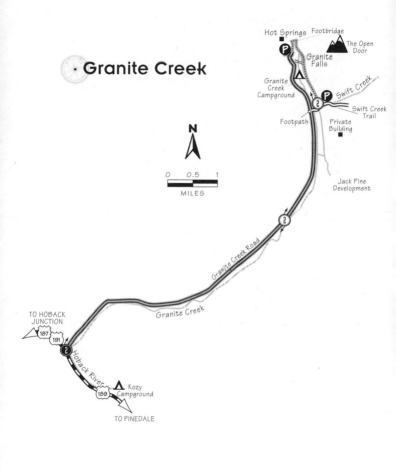

11.0 Trail comes to a trailhead parking area. Go through parking area and onto gravel road, turning right and over bridge.

11.2 Rejoin Granite Creek Road (FR 30530); turn left and return to start of ride.

18.9 Back at start.

Snake River Range

The first white men known to have seen the Snake River were the explorers Lewis and Clark in 1805. Clark named it Lewis River and early maps show it that way. In 1812 it was called Mad River because of all its cascades and falls. Later it was named Snake River for the Snake or Shoshone Indian tribes who lived there. The Snake River Range rises to the west, above the Snake River and forms a ribbon along the Wyoming-Idaho border. Four routes are described here but there are other trails and old logging roads worth exploring.

Falls Creek to Wilson Shuttle

Location: Immediately west of Hoback Junction and ending in the town of Wilson.

Distance: 18 miles one way.

Time: 3 to 4 hours.

Tread: Gravel road and paved road.

Season: This route is best in late spring through the fall.

Aerobic level: Moderate.

Technical difficulty: 2+

Hazards: Ruts and potholes in the gravel road; traffic on shoulderless paved road.

Highlights: Trail starts near Snake River Canyon, passes by Pritchard Creek, and climbs Pritchard Pass before descending and running adjacent to Falls Creek.

Land status: Bridger-Teton National Forest.

Maps: USGS Jackson, Munger Mountain, Teton Pass

Access: From Hoback Junction, turn west onto U.S. Highway 26-89. Continue past Astoria Hot Springs. About 4.5 miles from junction, turn right onto Falls Creek Road (Forest Road 31000).

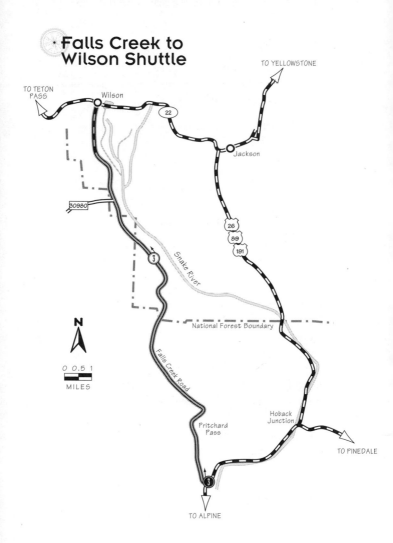

Falls Creek to Wilson Shuttle

TO YELLOWSTONE

TO TETON PASS

Wilson

22

Jackson

30980

3

Snake River

26

89

191

National Forest Boundary

N

0 0.5 1

MILES

Falls Creek Road

Hoback Junction

Pritchard Pass

TO PINEDALE

3

TO ALPINE

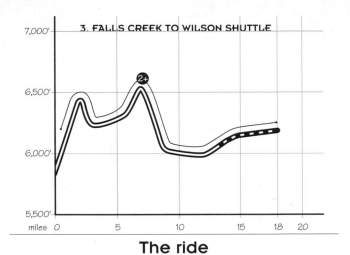

The ride

0.0 From intersection with US 26-89, go north on Falls Creek Road.

0.1 Pavement ends. Continue straight. Forest Service Work Station is on the right.

1.0 Cross cattleguard.

2.2 At top of long uphill.

3.1 Cross creek.

3.2 Road forks. Continue straight.

5.1 Road forks with a doubletrack going right. Continue on main road.

5.4 Cross cattleguard.

7.7 Cross cattleguard.

9.3 Cross cattleguard.

11.8 Start uphill climb.

12.1 Cross cattleguard as route levels out.

13.5 Cross creek. Road is paved on other side. This is a good ending point if you don't like riding in traffic on a narrow road.

18.0 At Wilson.

Dog Creek

Location: Snake River Canyon.

Distance: 7.2 miles out and back.

Time: 1.5 to 2.5 hours.

Tread: Mostly singletrack but some dirt road and double-track.

Season: From early summer into fall.

Aerobic level: Moderate with some short strenuous segments.

Technical difficulty: 2 on the dirt road and doubletrack; 3+ on the singletrack.

Hazards: Rocky segments, steep drop-offs, tree roots, logs and other debris; limited visibility in areas with thick vegetation.

Highlights: This scenic path parallels Dog Creek but the technical trail makes it difficult to sight-see while moving.

Land status: Targhee National Forest.

Maps: USGS Munger Mountain.

Access: At the Hoback Junction, take US 26-89 into Snake River Canyon. Continue past Astoria Hot Springs. About 4.5 miles from junction, you'll pass the entrance to Forest Road 31000. Continue 0.5 mile past Forest Road 31000 and turn right onto the dirt road. Park here (no camping is allowed). Another option is to continue 0.6 mile down highway to the Cabin Creek Campground and start the ride from there.

Dog Creek Trail

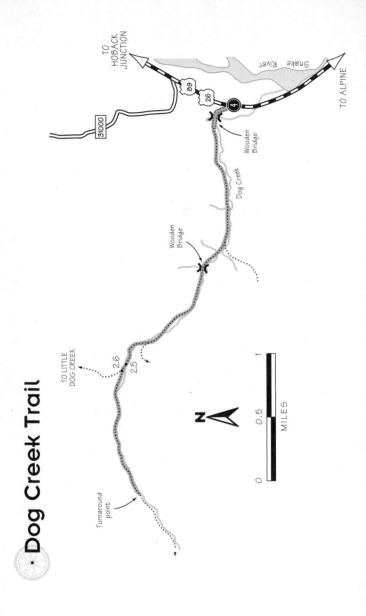

TO HOBACK JUNCTION

Snake River

TO ALPINE

31000

89

26

4

Wooden Bridge

Dog Creek

Wooden Bridge

TO LITTLE DOG CREEK

2.6

2.5

Turnaround point

N

0   0.5   1

MILES

Option: The route described here goes up Dog Creek to a point where the trail gets steep and bike riding becomes bike hiking. As an option, you can continue up the trail. It passes beneath Indian Peak (9,683 feet). Other route options are to take the trail to Cabin Creek, Little Dog Creek, or Pup Creek.

The ride

0.0 From parking area, follow road west.
0.1 Go over wooden bridge.
0.2 Trail intersection. Continue straight and follow trail marker. Trail becomes doubletrack.
0.4 Trail changes to singletrack.
0.6 Go through small creek—rock hop or ride through.
1.2 Hop over or ride through small creek.
2.0 Cross over wooden bridge that spans a ditch.
2.3 Wade across Dog Creek.
2.4 Trail forks. Continue straight on Dog Creek Trail. Left fork goes to Cabin Creek and is an optional route.
2.5 Wade across Dog Creek again.
2.6 Trail forks. Go left on Dog Creek Trail. Right follows the Little Dog Creek Trail and is another route to explore (it creates a loop with Pup Creek).

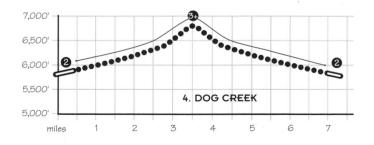

3.0 Pass through sagebrush clearing. Trail gets steeper after clearing.

3.6 Turnaround point is just before steep trail and creek crossing. Return for fun ride back to trailhead.

7.2 Back at start.

Mosquito Creek

Location: Southwest of Wilson in the Snake River Range.

Distance: 16.6 miles out and back.

Time: 2.5 to 4 hours.

Tread: Gravel road, singletrack and old logging roadbed.

Season: From early summer into fall.

Aerobic level: Moderate with some short strenuous segments.

Technical difficulty: 2 on gravel road; 3 to 4 on singletrack.

Hazards: Ruts and rocky areas; traffic; a 50-foot slide area at milepost 6.9 with rocks, boulders, and logs.

Highlights: The first part of the ride parallels Mosquito Creek, but the best part of the route is the singletrack that continues past the gravel road.

Land status: Bridger-Teton National Forest.

Maps: USGS Teton Pass, Palisades Peak.

Access: From Jackson, take Wyoming Highway 20 to Wilson. From Wilson, turn south onto Falls Creek Road and

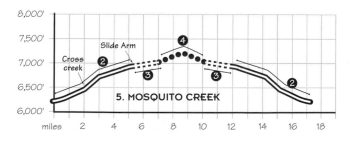

37

Mosquito Creek

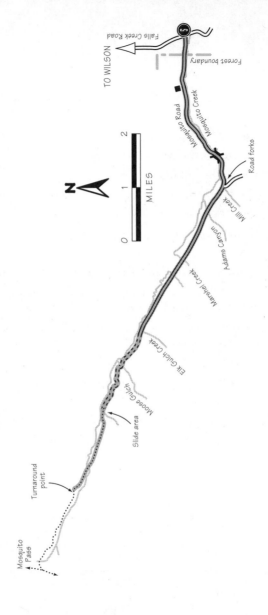

TO WILSON

Falls Creek Road

Forest boundary

Mosquito Road

Mosquito Creek

Road forks

Mill Creek

Adams Canyon

Marshal Creek

Elk Gulch Creek

Moose Gulch

Slide area

Turnaround point

Mosquito Pass

N

MILES

0   1   2

continue 4.4 miles to Mosquito Road. Turn right (west) and continue 0.6 mile to the forest boundary. The route starts here but there is dispersed camping all along Mosquito Road and the route can begin farther up the road.

The ride

0.0   Continue west down Mosquito Road.

0.4   Pass by house.

1.8   Pass over Mosquito Creek on wooden bridge.

1.9   ATV trail forks left. Continue on main road.

2.4   Road forks. Go right.

3.0   Pass over Adams Canyon Creek.

4.6   Doubletrack forks. Continue straight on main road. Right goes to outfitter camp.

5.3   Pass over Elk Gulch Creek (a culvert is in place). Go around ROAD CLOSED barricade. Route becomes less developed.

5.9   Doubletrack forks left. Continue straight and pass by Forest Service sign.

6.0   Road forks; stay left. Go over berm.

6.1   Pass over Moose Gulch Creek on wooden bridge. The route continues on a singletrack in an old logging roadbed.

6.9   Pass through slide area. The creek runs beneath the rock and log debris and you'll have to pick your way across the debris field. Singletrack path becomes rougher after creek.

7.8   Cross small creek.

8.3   Route ends at old mine site—a flat area in an old clearcut. The trail to Mosquito Pass continues up the hill but it is very rough and not suitable for biking. This is the turnaround point. Return on same route.

16.6   Back at starting point.

Smoky Hollow

Location: Southwest of Wilson, off Mosquito Creek Road in the Snake River Range.

Distance: 11 miles out and back.

Time: 2.5 to 3.5 hours.

Tread: Developed Forest Service road that has been closed due to damage.

Season: From early summer into fall.

Aerobic level: Moderate with some short strenuous segments.

Technical difficulty: Mostly 2+ with short segments of 3.

Hazards: Erosion gullies and rocky areas; watch for ATV and motorcycle traffic.

Highlights: No cars allowed; several options to explore other trails such as Observation Peak and Elk Creek Trail.

Land status: Bridger-Teton National Forest.

Maps: USGS Teton Pass.

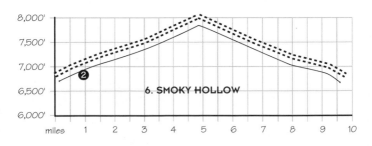

Smoky Hollow

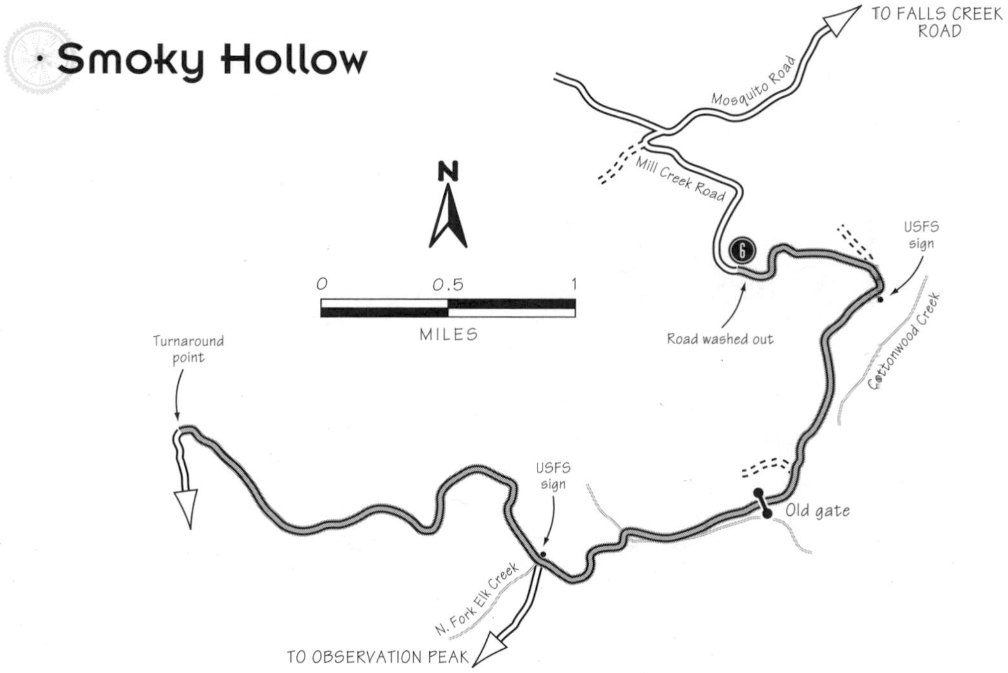

TO FALLS CREEK ROAD

Mosquito Road

Mill Creek Road

USFS sign

Cottonwood Creek

Road washed out

Old gate

N. FORK ELK CREEK

USFS sign

TO OBSERVATION PEAK

Turnaround point

N

0   0.5   1

MILES

Access: From Jackson, take Wyoming Highway 20 to Wilson. From Wilson, turn south onto Falls Creek Road and continue 4.4 miles to Mosquito Road. Turn right (west) and continue down Mosquito Road. Continue 3 miles to intersection and take left fork up the hill (Mill Creek Road). The road ends after 1.1 miles where road is damaged. Park at the barricade.

The ride

0.0	Walk around barricade on old road.
0.1	Walk bike around damaged area.
0.5	Doubletrack comes in on left; continue straight. This road comes up from main road below.
0.6	Pass by Forest Service sign that says COTTONWOOD CREEK.
1.6	Doubletrack forks right. Continue straight.
1.7	Pass by old gate.
2.7	Road forks; stay right.
2.8	Pass by Forest Service sign at head of Big Elk Creek. Go right.
4.9	Route follows curve and climbs up open area.
5.5	Reach summit. This is the turnaround point but trail continues west if you want to keep going. Return on same route.
11.0	Back at starting point.

Teton Pass

State Highway 22 rises west from Wilson and switchbacks its way to Teton Pass, going from an elevation of 6,100 feet to 8,431 feet within six miles. The Old Pass Road parallels the highway and offers a safe route up to the Pass. One-way rides from the Pass to Wilson are popular but both routes described here are done in loops that begin and end near Wilson. The Black Canyon route reaches Teton Pass and then follows a technical singletrack as it descends. The Phillips Canyon route also begins on the Old Pass Road but it heads north before reaching Teton Pass. Both are strenuous rides but one-way options can transform them into fast downhill rides.

Black Canyon Loop

Location: Teton Pass Area, south of State Highway 22.

Distance: 12-mile loop.

Time: 3 to 4 hours.

Tread: Deteriorating pavement, singletrack, and dirt road.

Season: From early summer into fall.

Aerobic level: Strenuous.

Technical difficulty: 2 on the route up to Teton Pass; 4 on the route down through Black Canyon.

Hazards: Traffic on State Highway 22; rocky segments and rough trail in Black Canyon.

Highlights: Nine miles of air-gasping uphill with six switchbacks followed by nearly 8 miles of steep downhill.

Land status: Bridger-Teton National Forest.

Maps: USGS Teton Pass.

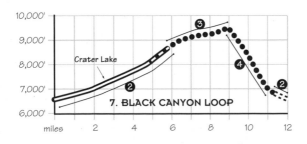

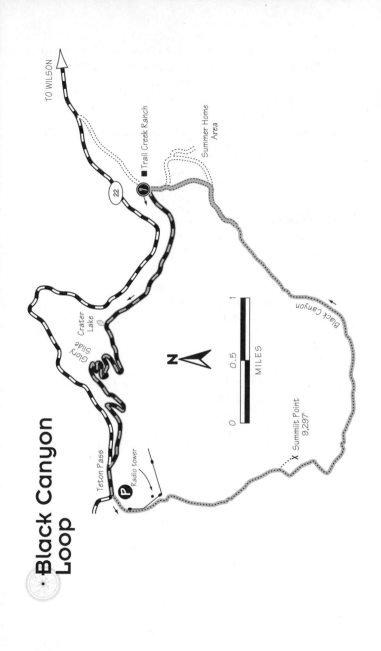

Black Canyon Loop

TO WILSON

22

Trail Creek Ranch

Summer Home Area

Crater Lake

Glory Slide

Black Canyon

N

MILES

0   0.5   1

Teton Pass

Radio tower

P

Summiit Point
9,297

Access: From Jackson, take State Highway 22 to Wilson. From Wilson continue up the highway toward Teton Pass for one mile. Turn left (south) at road leading to Trail Creek Ranch. Continue for one mile, past the Trail Creek Ranch, to end of road. Park here.

(If you prefer an easier ride, shuttle-start from the top of Teton Pass down to Wilson.)

The ride

0.0 Go around berm and start up Old Pass Road.

1.3 Pass by Crater Lake.

1.9 Road forks; continue straight. Old roadbed with singletrack path forks right and follows the Phillips Canyon Trail.

5.3 Merge onto State Highway 22.

5.5 At Teton Pass. Go through parking lot and take the service road leading south. Follow ridgeline on singletrack.

6.0 Pass by radio tower.

9.0 Near summit point (9,279 feet), bear right at fork at log/bench. Begin downhill.

11.0 Path upgrades to dirt road.

12.0 Back at starting point.

Phillips Canyon Loop

Location: Teton Pass Area, south and then north of State Highway 22.

Distance: 15.5 miles.

Time: 4 to 5 hours.

Tread: Deteriorating pavement; singletrack, and dirt road.

Season: From early summer into fall.

Aerobic level: Strenuous.

Technical difficulty: 2 on the route up to Teton Pass; 3+ on the route up to and through Phillips Canyon; 1+ on the final five miles of pavement.

Hazards: Traffic on State Highway 22; rocky segments and rough trail with roots and logs on the route through Phillips Canyon.

Highlights: Five miles of air-gasping uphill to the top of Phillips Canyon; technically tricky and exciting ride through Phillips Canyon.

Land status: Bridger-Teton National Forest.

Maps: USGS Teton Pass, Teton Village.

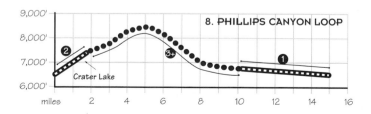

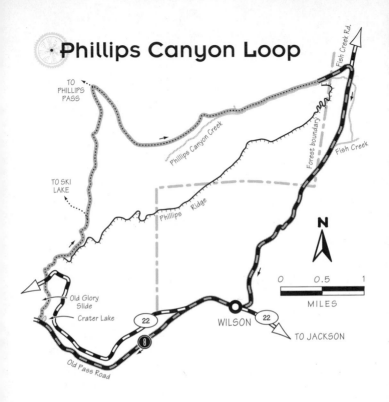

Phillips Canyon Loop

TO PHILLIPS PASS

Phillips Canyon Creek

Fish Creek Rd.

Forest boundary

Fish Creek

TO SKI LAKE

Phillips   Ridge

N

Old Glory Slide

Crater Lake

22

WILSON

22

0   0.5   1

MILES

TO JACKSON

8

Old Pass Road

Access: From Jackson, take State Highway 22 to Wilson. From Wilson continue up the highway toward Teton Pass for one mile. Turn left (south) at road leading to Trail Creek Ranch. Continue for one mile, past the Trail Creek Ranch, to end of road. Park here.

The ride

0.0   Go around berm and start up Old Pass Road.
1.3   Pass by Crater Lake.
1.7   Take first switchback up the trail.

1.9	Road forks on second switchback. Take right fork and continue on old roadbed with singletrack. Continue through Old Glory Slide.
2.7	Come to State Highway 22. Turn left onto highway and then immediately take right turn onto dirt road.
3.0	Road forks. Go left onto singletrack.
3.1	Trail forks. Go left toward Ski Lake and Phillips Pass.
3.7	At ridgeline. Great view.
3.9	Trail forks; continue straight. Left goes to Ski Lake.
4.8	Start decent.
5.5	Cross small creek.
5.6	Cross small creek.
5.7	Trail forks. Go right past sign. Left goes to Phillips Pass. Trail becomes rougher.
8.0	Cross North Fork of Phillips Canyon Creek.
8.7	Cross creek, back and forth.
9.5	Cross a primitive road and continue straight. Cross the creek. Brief segment of private property. Stay on trail.
9.9	Come to paved Fish Creek Road. Turn right onto road and return to Wilson.
13.0	Stop at stop sign and turn right onto Main Street.
13.4	Turn right onto State Highway 22.
14.5	Turn left at Heidelburg on road to Trail Creek Ranch.
15.5	Back at start.

Jackson Town Area

You don't have to go far from Jackson to find great single-track or dirt road pedaling. One advantage of having national forest lands adjacent to the city limits is the opportunity for scenic cycling right from town. The Cache Creek area is a popular recreation spot for the local residents and it can get busy. The three routes described follow Cache Creek on an old gravel road that has been closed to motorized travel. The Putt-Putt and Tiny Hagen Trails parallel the Cache Creek Trail, on opposite sides of the creek, and they offer singletrack options to biking the main gravel road. Mix and match the trails as it suits your fancy.

Cache Creek to Game Creek Loop

Location: Immediately southeast of the town of Jackson.

Distance: 18-mile loop.

Time: 3 to 4 hours.

Tread: Dirt road, singletrack, and pavement.

Season: This route is best in late spring through the fall.

Aerobic level: Moderate.

Technical difficulty: 3 overall with some sections of 1, 2, and 4.

Hazards: Steep and rocky segments on Game Creek Trail; traffic on U.S. Highway 26-89-191.

Highlights: An entertaining ride as it heads up Cache Creek; striking views of the Gros Ventre Range and Snake River Valley.

Land status: Bridger-Teton National Forest and U.S. Highway.

Maps: USGS Jackson, Cache Creek.

Access: In Jackson, from U.S. Highway 26-89-191 on the west end of town, turn south at intersection with Maple Way. At **T** intersection, turn left onto Scott and then take an immediate right onto Snow King Avenue. Turn left onto Vine and, at a stop sign, turn right onto Kelly Avenue. Turn right onto Redmond and immediately left onto Cache

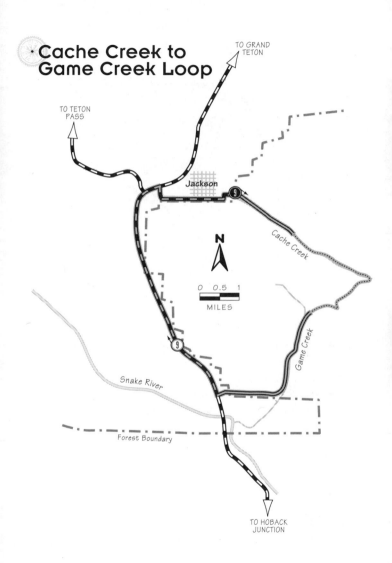

Cache Creek to Game Creek Loop

TO GRAND TETON

TO TETON PASS

Jackson

9

Cache Creek

N

0   0.5   1
MILES

9

Game Creek

Snake River

Forest Boundary

TO HOBACK JUNCTION

Creek Drive. Pavement ends at the forest service boundary and turns into Forest Road 30450. After about a half mile, road ends at parking area. Park here.

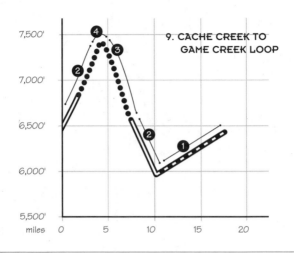

9. CACHE CREEK TO GAME CREEK LOOP

The ride

0.0 From parking area, go to east side and onto road following Cache Creek.

0.4 Road forks. Stay left. Right goes to a private site.

1.9 At trailhead. Gate over trail may, or may not, be closed. Go past or around it. Trail goes to single-track.

3.7 Cross creek on a good wooden bridge.

3.9 Trail forks. Go right across good bridge onto Game Creek Trail and start up steep and rocky hill.

4.6 Come to saddle and start downhill.

7.3 Pass by pond to the right.

7.5 Trail joins Game Creek Road.

9.6 Road forks. Go right onto dirt road and downhill.

10.6 Come to intersection with paved US 189-191. Shuttle route ends here and avoids pavement and heavy traffic. To continue on loop, turn right and return to start via the highway.

18.0 Back at start of ride.

Putt-Putt

Location: Immediately southeast of the town of Jackson.

Distance: 4.7-mile loop.

Time: 45 minutes to 1 hour.

Tread: Dirt road and singletrack.

Season: Best from late spring through fall, but it can be ridden whenever there isn't snow on the ground.

Aerobic level: Easy to moderate.

Technical difficulty: 2 on the dirt road; 3 on the actual Putt-Putt Trail.

Hazards: Deep ruts in the singletrack that leave little room to maneuver; steep rocky sections and wet stream crossings.

Highlights: Imagine combining a roller-coaster ride and a bobsled run—the result would be the Putt-Putt loop.

Land status: Bridger-Teton National Forest.

Maps: USGS Cache Creek.

Access: In Jackson, from U.S. Highway 26-89-191, on the west end of town, turn south at the intersection with Maple Way. At the **T** intersection, turn left onto Scott and then take an immediate right onto Snow King Avenue. Turn left onto Vine and, at a stop sign, turn right onto Kelly Avenue. Turn right onto Redmond and then take an immediate left onto Cache Creek Drive. Pavement ends at the forest service boundary where the road turns into Forest Road 30450.

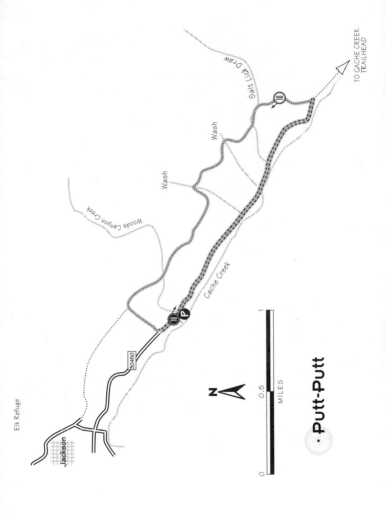

Elk Refuge

Jackson

Woods Canyon Creek

Salt Lick Draw

Wash

Wash

Cache Creek

30450

TO CACHE CREEK
TRAILHEAD

N

0   0.5   1
MILES

· Putt-Putt

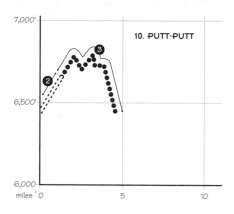

10. PUTT-PUTT

After about a half mile, the road ends at a parking area. Park here.

Option: At mile 4.3, continue on trail into town

The ride

0.0 From parking area, go to east side and onto road following Cache Creek.
0.4 Road forks. Stay left. Right goes to a private site.
1.4 Trail forks. Go left on steep uphill trail, marked with Putt-Putt Trail sign. Straight continues up Cache Creek Trail.
1.6 At top of steep segment. Trail becomes a series of up-and-down runs from one wash to the next.
4.0 Start steep downhill.
4.3 Trail forks. Go left. Right continues route on into town.
4.4 Trail forks. Go right.
4.5 Come out onto gravel FR 30450. Turn left.
4.7 Back at parking area.

Tiny Hagen Trail

Location: Immediately adjacent to Jackson town limits on Cache Creek.

Distance: 4.5-mile loop.

Time: 1 to 1.5 hours.

Tread: Singletrack and dirt road.

Season: Best from late spring through the fall but it can be ridden whenever there isn't snow on the ground.

Aerobic level: Easy.

Technical difficulty: 2 for the first 1.5 miles; 3 on the Tiny Hagen singletrack trail.

Hazards: Rocky areas and rutted segments.

Highlights: Fun, up-and-down action; creek crossings on good bridges.

Land status: Bridger-Teton National Forest.

Maps: USGS Cache Creek.

Access: In Jackson, from U.S. Highway 26-89-191 on the west end of town, turn south at intersection with Maple Way. At the **T** intersection, turn left onto Scott and then take an immediate right onto Snow King Avenue. Turn left onto Vine and, at a stop sign, turn right onto Kelly Avenue. Turn right onto Redmond and immediately left onto Cache Creek Drive. Pavement ends at the forest service boundary where the road turns into Forest Road 30450. After about a half mile, road ends at parking area. Park here. Trail starts approximately 100 feet before parking area.

The ride

0.0 From parking area, continue across lot to the east side and onto road following Cache Creek.

0.4 Road forks. Stay left. Right goes to a private site.

1.4 Trail forks. Continue straight. Left follows Putt-Putt Trail.

1.6 Trail comes in from right. Continue straight.

1.9 Pass by gate on trail. Trail becomes singletrack.

2.1 Trail forks. Go right onto Tiny Hagen Trail. Cross creek. Trail goes in and out of forest and crosses Cache Creek five times. Trail is marked with blue diamonds.

4.4 Come out onto main Forest Road 30450. Turn right and return to parking area.

4.5 Back at start.

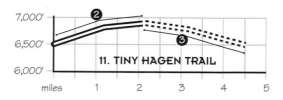

Tiny Hagen Trail

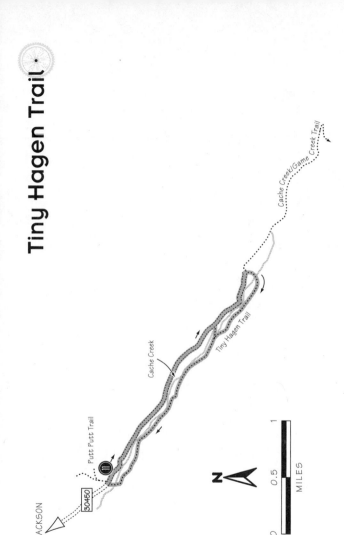

TO JACKSON

30450

Putt Putt Trail

Cache Creek

Cache Creek/Game Creek Trail

Tiny Hagen Trail

N

0   0.5   1

MILES

Elk Refuge

The National Elk Refuge is a spectacular sight in the winter when it becomes home to 7,500 elk. The refuge was created in 1912 as a result of public interest in the survival of the elk herd and covers nearly 25,000 acres. It is comprised of meadows and marshes along the valley floor and sagebrush and rock outcroppings along the foothills. Elk are on the refuge for about six months, typically from November to April, and supplemental feed is provided for two to three months, depending on the severity of the weather.

There are only two routes in this section on the refuge itself: The Elk Refuge Trail and Flat Creek Road. The others are on nearby national forest lands. There is no overnight parking or camping on the refuge but there are areas for dispersed camping on national forest lands. A campground is located near Curtis Canyon.

Flat Creek Road

Location: Immediately east of Jackson.

Distance: 27 miles out and back.

Time: 4 to 6 hours.

Tread: Improved gravel road and unimproved gravel road.

Season: From late spring and into fall. Weather may permit use earlier in the spring.

Aerobic level: Easy.

Technical difficulty: Mostly 2 with some sections of 3.

Hazards: Traffic; rough and rocky sections near Flat Lake.

Highlights: A nice leisurely ride from town.

Land status: National Elk Refuge, Bridger-Teton National Forest.

Maps: USGS Cache Creek, Gros Ventre Junction, Blue Miner Lake.

Access: In Jackson, follow Broadway Street east to the end of town. Park at entrance to National Elk Refuge.

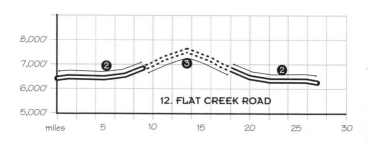

Flat Creek Road

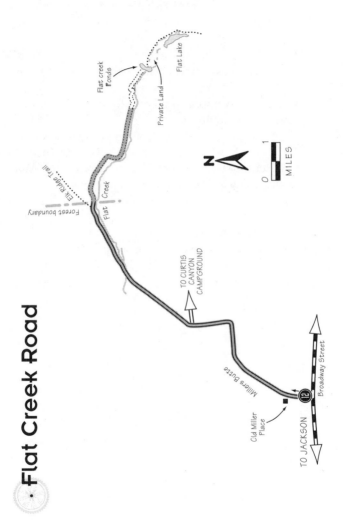

Flat Creek Ponds

Flat Lake

Private Land

Elk Ridge Trail

Forest Boundary

Flat Creek

N

0   1

MILES

TO CURTIS CANYON CAMPGROUND

Miller Butte

Old Miller Place

12

Broadway Street

TO JACKSON

The ride

0.0 Begin at entrance to the elk refuge.

0.7 Pass by Old Miller Place.

4.3 Road becomes rougher with end of county maintenance.

4.7 Junction; continue straight. Right goes to Curtis Canyon Campground.

7.0 Cross over creek. After crossing, go right.

9.0 Road to left is closed to motorized travel (it is the Elk Refuge Trail). Cross into national forest lands where road is less developed and rocky. This is a good turnaround point for those wanting a shorter ride.

10.4 Begin to drop down to creek.

12.6 Bike hike across river cobble area.

13.5 Come to Flat Creek Ponds and turnaround point. Return on same route.

27.0 Back at start.

13

Elk Refuge Trail

Location: Approximately 9 miles east of the town of Jackson beginning on the National Elk Refuge.

Distance: 4.8 miles out and back.

Time: 1 hour plus optional hiking time.

Tread: Doubletrack with some short sections of singletrack.

Season: From late spring and into fall.

Aerobic level: Easy, turning moderate near the turnaround point.

Technical difficulty: 2 and 3.

Hazards: The trail is overgrown in some areas, making the road surface hard to see.

Highlights: Crosses grassland prairie of the National Elk Refuge and then enters the Bridger-Teton National Forest. As a bonus to your ride, leave your bike at the turnaround point and hike up the trail for an even better view of the Tetons.

Land status: National Elk Refuge, Bridger-Teton National Forest.

Maps: USGS Blue Miner Lake.

Access: In Jackson, follow Broadway Street east to the end of town. Take the Elk Refuge Road for 8.9 miles. At the fork at mile 4.8, continue straight on Flat Creek Road for another 4.4 miles. Park in small lot adjacent to ROAD CLOSED TO MOTORIZED VEHICLES sign.

Elk Refuge Trail

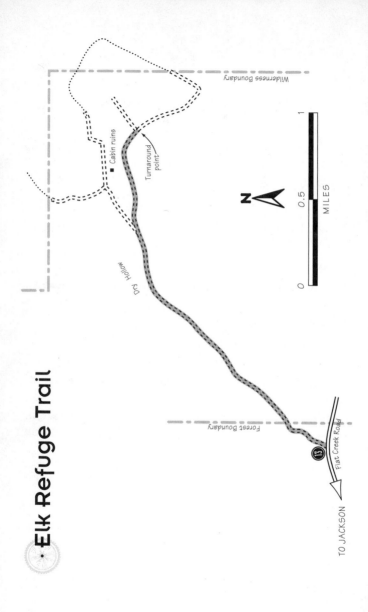

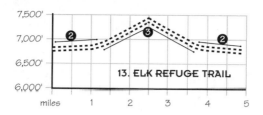

The ride

0.0 Go around ROAD CLOSED TO MOTORIZED VEHICLES sign and follow doubletrack.

0.4 Pass National Elk Refuge Boundary signs.

1.0 Trail forks; continue straight.

1.6 Faint doubletrack forks right; continue straight.

1.7 Trail forks; go right.

1.9 Pass by barricade next to the road.

2.4 See a forest service trail marker. This is the turn-around point for the bike route but the trail continues and, in about 0.5 mile, enters the Gros Ventre Wilderness Area.

4.8 Back at starting point.

Curtis Canyon Trail

Location: Approximately 12 miles east of the town of Jackson above the National Elk Refuge.

Distance: 3.2 miles out and back.

Time: 40 minutes to 1 hour.

Tread: ATV trail, doubletrack and singletrack.

Season: From late spring into fall.

Aerobic Level: Moderate.

Technical difficulty: 2

Hazards: Rocky areas and muddy holes. Nearly all of the stream crossings go over culverts.

Highlights: A nice evening or early morning ride, especially if you're staying in the campground. It's a pretty ride as it meanders back and forth across the creek.

Land status: Bridger-Teton National Forest.

Maps: USGS Gros Ventre Junction.

Access: In Jackson, follow Broadway Street east to the end of town. Take the Elk Refuge Road for 4.5 miles and turn

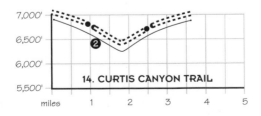

· Curtis Canyon Trail

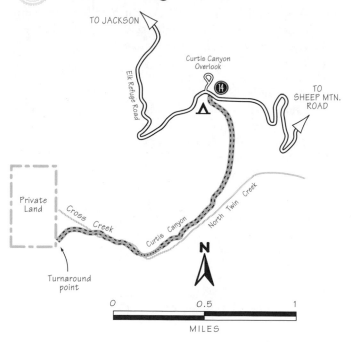

TO JACKSON

Curtis Canyon
Overlook

Elk Refuge Road

14

⛺

TO
SHEEP MTN.
ROAD

Private
Land

Cross Creek

Curtis Canyon

North Twin Creek

Turnaround
point

N

0   0.5   1

MILES

right (east) onto the road to Curtis Canyon Campground. Park in campground. The route starts on the road immediately east of the campground.

The ride

0.0 Head south on doubletrack that parallels the campground. It turns into singletrack from time to time.

0.8 Cross creek and trail becomes singletrack.

0.9 Trail widens into ATV trail.

1.2 Pass over creek.

1.4 Pass over creek.

1.6 Reach turnaround point at fence that borders private land. Return on same route.

3.2 Back at starting point.

Sheep Creek Road
Out-and-Back

Location: Approximately 12 miles east of the town of Jackson above the National Elk Refuge.

Distance: 8.4 miles out and back.

Time: 1 to 2 hours.

Tread: Good gravel road and a short section of doubletrack.

Season: From late spring into fall.

Aerobic level: Moderate to strenuous.

Technical difficulty: 2

Hazards: Scattered pockets of dense gravel, some traffic.

Highlights: Outstanding view of the Tetons from the summit on Sheep Mountain.

Land status: Bridger-Teton National Forest.

Maps: USGS Gros Ventre Junction, Blue Miner Lake.

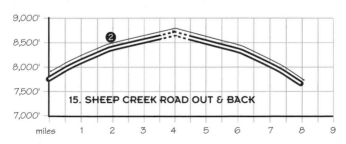

15. SHEEP CREEK ROAD OUT & BACK

Access: In town, follow Broadway Street east to the end of town. Take the Elk Refuge Road for 4.5 miles and turn right (east) onto the road to Curtis Canyon Campground. After 7.2 miles, pass by the campground. After 1.8 miles, the road forks. Take the left fork onto the Sheep Creek Road and go another 1.3 miles. Park in small parking area near monument.

Option: If you prefer a less developed route off the mountain, follow the second half of Sheep Creek Loop (Ride 16).

The ride

0.0   From parking area, continue following the main Sheep Mountain Road.
0.4   Closed road forks off to left (route for Sheep Creek Loop, Ride 16).
1.9   Another closed road forks off to left (north).
2.9   Road becomes rougher.
3.5   Near summit. Just before the lookout point, go right on doubletrack that continues north and drops down into a drainage. This is a pleasant little segment that passes through the woods.
4.2   Road ends abruptly. Turn around here. On the way back, take the time to stop at the summit overlook and then return on same route.
8.4   Back at starting point.

Sheep Creek

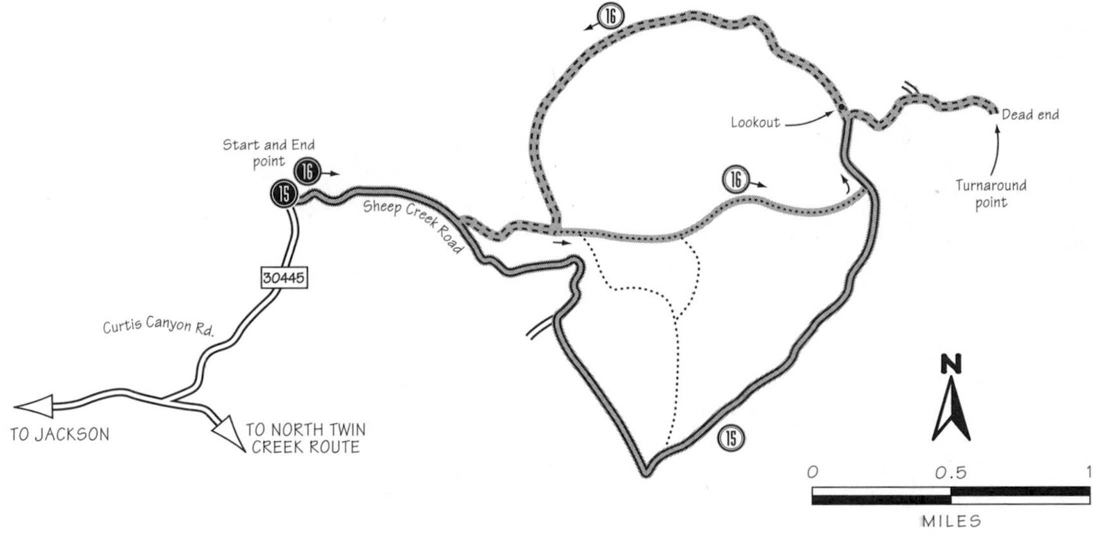

Dead end

Turnaround point

Lookout

16

16

15

15

16

Start and End point

Sheep Creek Road

30445

Curtis Canyon Rd.

TO JACKSON

TO NORTH TWIN CREEK ROUTE

N

0   0.5   1

MILES

Sheep Creek Loop

See map on page 75.

Location: Approximately 12 miles east of the town of Jackson above the National Elk Refuge.

Distance: 4.8 miles.

Time: 1.5 to 2.5 hours.

Tread: Gravel road, singletrack and doubletrack.

Season: From late spring into fall.

Aerobic level: Strenuous.

Technical difficulty: 4 on the way up, 2+ coming down.

Hazards: At times the trail can be difficult to recognize; some bike hiking is required when the trail becomes nondescript at mile 1.8. Don't count on water in the creek late in the summer.

Highlights: Outstanding view of the Tetons from the summit on Sheep Mountain. The route is open only to nonmotorized travel.

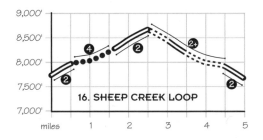

Land status: Bridger-Teton National Forest.

Maps: USGS Gros Ventre Junction, Blue Miner Lake.

Access: In Jackson, follow Broadway Street east to the end of town. Take the Elk Refuge Road for 4.5 miles and turn right (east) onto the road to Curtis Canyon Campground. After 7.2 miles, pass by campground. After another 1.8 miles, the road forks. Take the left fork onto the Sheep Creek Road and go another 1.3 miles. Park in small parking area near monument.

The ride

0.0 From the parking area, continue following the main Sheep Mountain Road up the mountain.

0.4 Take left fork at ROAD CLOSED sign. (Sheep Mountain Road Trail continues on gravel road.) Go around sign and barricade and drop into drainage.

0.6 Reach the bottom of the draw, and then start up again.

0.9 Trail forks. Take faint trail that goes left.

1.2 Drainage forks. Go left. Right is an option that connects with the main Sheep Mountain Road; it passes by a spring after 0.2 mile.

1.5 Trail gets less distinct.

1.8 Trail disappears altogether for a short stretch. Just ride (or walk) parallel to the drainage bottom, going up the hill.

2.1 Come out onto main Sheep Mountain Road. Go left and continue up the mountain.

2.6 Reach the lookout with beautiful view of the Tetons. Continue straight on doubletrack and go past the NO MOTORIZED TRAVEL sign.

3.0 Enter timber.

3.3 Road forks; go right into sagebrush opening.

4.0 Join another doubletrack road. Continue straight.

4.4 Back at road fork with ROAD CLOSED sign. Return on main road.

4.8 Back at start.

North Twin Creek Out-and-Back

Location: Immediately east of the town of Jackson.

Distance: 5.7 miles.

Time: 1 to 2 hours.

Tread: Doubletrack.

Season: From late spring and into fall.

Aerobic level: Moderate.

Technical difficulty: 2+

Hazards: Several obnoxiously rocky segments.

Highlights: Scenic views; wild raspberries; good training in trail literacy—learning to pick a good line on a fairly rocky road.

Land status: Bridger-Teton National Forest.

Maps: USGS Gros Ventre Junction, Cache Creek.

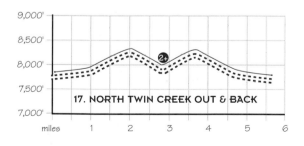

· North Twin Creek

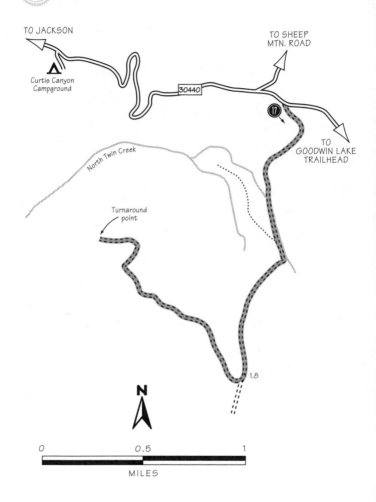

TO JACKSON

Curtis Canyon
Campground

30440

TO SHEEP
MTN. ROAD

17

TO
GOODWIN LAKE
TRAILHEAD

North Twin Creek

Turnaround
point

1.8

N

0   0.5   1

MILES

Access: In Jackson, follow Broadway Street east to the end of town. Take the Elk Refuge Road for 4.5 miles and turn right (east) on the road to Curtis Canyon Campground. After 7.2 miles, pass by the campground. After another 1.6 miles, the road forks. Take right fork and continue 0.4 mile and turn right onto doubletrack road. Park near beginning of road.

The ride

0.0 Take doubletrack road south from the main road.

0.5 Curve in road.

1.2 Cross creek. It may be dry late in the season.

1.8 Trail forks at major intersection. Go right. Left continues up the hill and dead-ends.

2.6 Trail forks; go left. Right goes into an old clearcut and provides a great view of the Tetons.

2.7 Come into old clearcut with great view of Tetons and the valley below. This is the turnaround point. Return on same route.

5.7 Back at start of route.

Gros Ventre

Gros Ventre, pronounced "Gro-vont," is French for *big bellies*. The name was given to the Arapaho Indian tribe, not because of their girth, but from their sign of gesturing with both hands in front of their stomachs to indicate when they were hungry.

The Gros Ventre River and the surrounding valley is wildly scenic. Red hills rise above the river and forested mountainsides lead to the Gros Ventre Wilderness Area. The valley also has some unique geology, most notably the Gros Ventre Slide.

In the spring of 1925, after several days of heavy rains and rapid snow melt, the north slope of Sheep Mountain (Sleeping Indian) collapsed, damming the Gros Ventre River. Lower Slide Lake, a five-mile-long lake, formed behind the dam. Two years later, the river broke through the dam and the resulting flood nearly obliterated the town of Kelly.

Two rides described here require fording the Gros Ventre River: The Grizzly Lake Adventure Loop and the Slate Creek route. Both could be tricky crossing early in the season. The beginning of the Gros Ventre River Easy Out-and-Back route borders the Gros Ventre River so don't be surprised if early in the season you discover the trail to be underwater.

Gros Ventre Road

Location: In the Gros Ventre River Valley.

Distance: 40 miles out and back.

Time: 6 to 8 hours.

Tread: Pavement and good gravel road.

Season: From spring into fall.

Aerobic level: Easy.

Technical difficulty: 2+

Hazards: Traffic on the narrow shoulderless paved road; sections of washboarded gravel road.

Highlights: Paralleling the Gros Ventre River and passing by the Gros Ventre Slide Lake; red cliffs bordering the valley past the lake.

Land status: Grand Teton National Park, Bridger-Teton National Forest.

Maps: USGS Gros Ventre Junction, Shadow Mountain, Mount Leidy, Grizzly Lake.

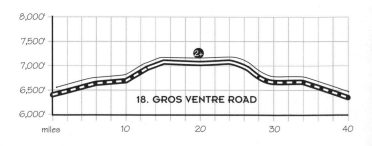

Gros Ventre Road

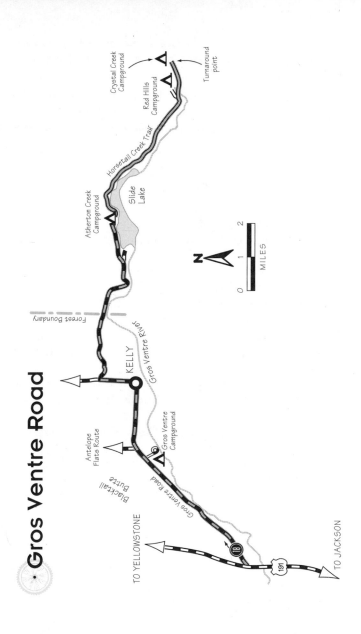

Access: From Jackson, take U.S. Highway 191 into Grand Teton National Park. Seven miles north of Jackson, turn right at Gros Ventre Junction and park near the junction.

Option: Your ride can start and turn around at any point on the route. The route described here ends at the Crystal Creek Campground but the route can continue for another 19 miles.

The ride

0.0   From the junction go east along Gros Ventre Road.

4.5   Road forks; continue straight. Right goes to Gros Ventre Campground.

4.6   Mormon Road (part of Antelope Flats Route) goes left; continue straight.

6.4   Pass by the little community of Kelly. Pass by small store on south side of road.

7.6   Road forks. Go right (east) on Gros Ventre Road.

10.9 Exit Grand Teton National Park and enter National Forest.

11.0 Kelly Warm Springs is next to the river on the right.

13.4 Pass by overlook with information kiosk. Begin passing Slide Lake.

14.1 Right goes to Atherton Creek Campground. Stay straight as pavement ends.

15.8 Pass by trailhead to Horsetail Creek Route (on left).

19.6 Pass by Red Hills Campground and trailhead to Grizzly Lake Trail Route.

20.0 Come to Crystal Creek Campground on the left. This is the turnaround point. Road continues and comes to Upper Slide Lake in 6.9 miles. Return by same route.

40.0 Back at starting point.

Gros Ventre River Easy Out-and-Back

Location: In the Gros Ventre River Valley.

Distance: 3.6 miles.

Time: 30 to 60 minutes.

Tread: Doubletrack with a very short section of singletrack.

Season: Best in summer, after the spring runoff. During periods of heavy runoff, the start of the trail may be under water.

Aerobic level: Easy.

Technical difficulty: 2+

Hazards: Narrow path along river at start of ride; sections of rocky areas; easy creek crossings. The trail drops down to the river's edge and may be hard to follow in spring and early summer during spring runoff.

Highlights: A fun little ride that follows along the Gros Ventre River before it heads across the sagebrush prairie.

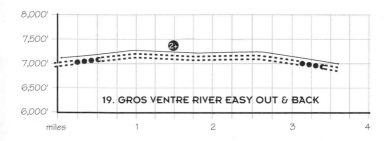

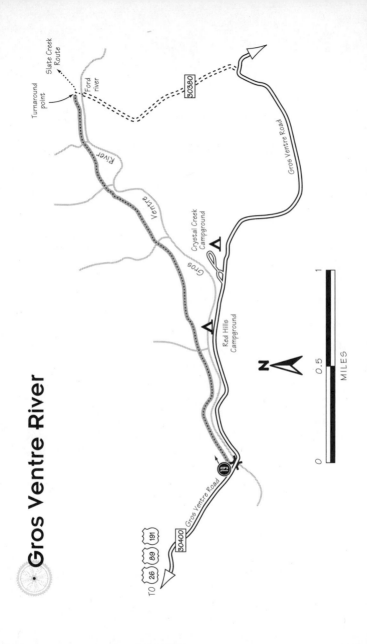

Gros Ventre River

Land status: Bridger-Teton National Forest.

Maps: USGS Grizzly Lake.

Access: From Jackson, go north on U.S. Highway 26-89-191 for 7 miles. At Gros Ventre Junction, turn right (east) on Gros Ventre Road. Continue down road for about 18 miles. Just before the bridge that crosses over Gros Ventre River, turn left (north) onto doubletrack. Park here.

Option: This route can be connected with the Slate Creek Trail to eliminate the wet crossing of the river for that route.

The ride

0.0 Follow doubletrack along west bank of river.
0.1 Drop down onto singletrack that goes along river-bank.
0.2 Trail leaves river edge and is easier to pedal. The trail passes through several draws, which may have some runoff early in the season.
1.0 Cross little creek
1.3 Trail begins descent to river.
1.8 Trail ends. Turn around or continue on Slate Creek Trail.
3.6 Back at start.

Red Hills Campground Loop

Location: Gros Ventre River Valley.

Distance: 3.5 miles.

Time: 1 to 1.5 hours.

Tread: Singletrack and doubletrack.

Season: From late spring through fall.

Aerobic level: Moderate.

Technical difficulty: 2+ to 3.

Hazards: Narrow, rocky singletrack.

Highlights: Roller-coaster singletrack; scenic doubletrack with great view of the Tetons.

Land status: Bridger-Teton National Forest.

Maps: USGS Grizzly Lake.

Access: From Jackson, go north on U.S. Highway 26-89-191 for 7 miles. At Gros Ventre Junction, turn right (east)

Red Hills Campground Loop

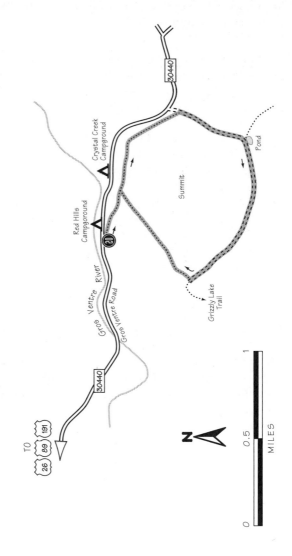

on Gros Ventre Road. Continue down road for 19.6 miles to Red Hills Campground. Trailhead parking is just before turnoff into campground.

Option: An easy option is to drop down to the road before the doubletrack and return to the campground on the gravel road.

The ride

0.0   Take trail that goes south from trailhead parking area.
0.2   Trail forks; go right.
0.4   Trail forks; go left.
0.6   Trail joins doubletrack. Continue straight.
0.8   Trail forks. Go right onto singletrack. The trail parallels the main Gros Ventre Road. It forks several times; always stay right.
1.3   At wooden sign, continue right.
1.4   Intersect with old doubletrack. Go right and go around hill.
1.7   Pass under powerline.
1.8   Pass by small pond.
1.9   Go though gate and continue straight. Teton Mountains will come into view in about 100 yards.
2.8   Intersect hiking trail. To complete loop, turn right.
3.5   Back at trailhead.

Grizzly Lake
Out-and-Back

Location: Gros Ventre River Valley.

Distance: 7.8 miles.

Time: 2 to 3 hours.

Tread: Singletrack.

Season: This route is best in late spring through the fall.

Aerobic level: Moderate to strenuous.

Technical difficulty: 3+

Hazards: Rocky segments and areas with logs and roots and other debris; yield to hikers and horseback riders.

Highlights: Several roller-coaster sections and creek crossings; a peaceful lake that is a great place to relax for lunch.

Land status: Bridger-Teton National Forest.

Maps: USGS Grizzly Lake.

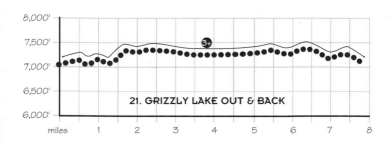

Grizzly Lake

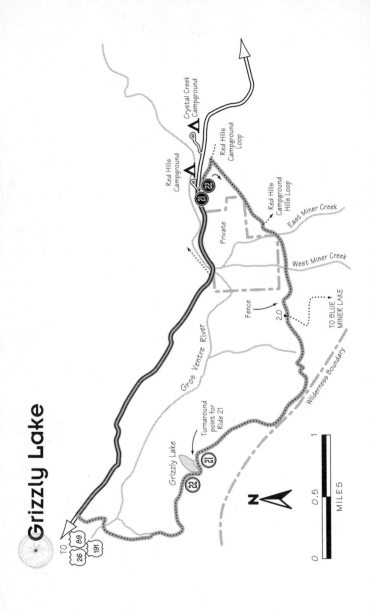

Access: From Jackson, go north on U.S. Highway 26-89-191 for seven miles. At Gros Ventre Junction, turn right (east) on Gros Ventre Road. Continue down road for 19.6 miles to Red Hills Campground. Trailhead parking is just before turnoff into campground.

The ride

0.0 Take trail south from trailhead parking area.
0.2 Trail forks; go right.
0.4 Trail forks; go right.
0.6 Trail forks; continue straight.
0.7 Cross creek on wooden bridge.
0.8 Cross creek on single log bridge or wade across. Hike up hill after crossing.
1.0 At top of hill.
1.3 Cross West Miner Creek. Trail forks after creek; stay left.
1.4 Cross little creek. Trail forks after creek; stay straight. Left goes to cabin.
1.5 At top of ridge.
1.7 Cross little stream.
1.9 Pass by fence with old gate.
2.0 Pass by trail sign. Continue straight. Left goes to Blue Miner Lake.
2.3 Cross small stream.
2.6 Reach top of ridge and begin easy downhill.
3.8 Trail forks. Go right.
3.9 At Grizzly Lake and turnaround point. Return by same route.
7.8 Back at trailhead.

Grizzly Lake
Adventure Loop

See map on page 94.

Location: Gros Ventre River Valley.

Distance: 8.6 miles.

Time: 3 to 5 hours.

Tread: Singletrack and gravel road.

Season: From late spring through fall.

Aerobic level: Moderate, easy on gravel road

Technical difficulty: 3+ to 4 on singletrack; 2 on gravel road.

Hazards: Rocky segments and areas with logs and roots and other debris; deadfall that requires picking the bike up and over each log; wet river crossings that may be difficult during periods of high runoff.

Highlights: Challenging sections through the deadfall; swift river crossing; scenic Grizzly Lake.

Land Status: Bridger-Teton National Forest.

Maps: USGS Grizzly Lake.

Access: From Jackson, go north on U.S. Highway 26-89-191 for 7 miles. At Gros Ventre Junction, turn right (east) on Gros Ventre Road. Continue down road for 19.6 miles to Red Hills Campground. Trailhead parking is just before turnoff into campground.

The ride

0.0 Take trail from trailhead parking area.
0.2 Trail forks; go right.
0.4 Trail forks; go right.
0.6 Trail forks; continue straight.
0.7 Cross creek on wooden bridge.
0.8 Cross creek on single log bridge or wade across. Hike up hill after crossing.
1.0 At top of hill.
1.3 Cross West Miner Creek. Trail forks after creek; stay left.
1.4 Cross little creek. Trail forks after creek; stay straight. Left goes to cabin.
1.5 At top of ridge.
1.7 Cross little stream.
1.9 Pass by fence with old gate.
2.0 Pass by trail sign. Continue straight. Left goes to Blue Miner Lake.
2.3 Cross small stream..
2.6 Reach top of ridge and begin easy downhill.
3.8 Trail forks. Go right.
3.9 At Grizzly Lake.
4.7 Pass by fence (there is no gate). From this point the trail is blocked repeatedly by deadfall where you must hoist your bike over the debris.

4.8	At Redmond Creek.
4.9	Cross creek.
6.6	Trail forks; go right.
6.7	Wade across the Gros Ventre River. Trail picks up on other side. If you miss the trail, bushwhack up to road.
7.1	On Gros Ventre Road. Go right.
7.7	Cross river on bridge.
8.6	Back at trailhead.

Slate Creek

Location: Gros Ventre River Valley.

Distance: 8.2 miles out and back.

Time: 2 to 4 hours.

Tread: Doubletrack with several narrow sections.

Season: From late spring through the fall. Avoid this ride during periods of high runoff.

Aerobic Level: Moderate.

Technical difficulty: 2+ to 3.

Hazards: Fording the Gros Ventre River, although the crossing is easy except during periods of high runoff; creek crossings and muddy segments that require bike hiking.

Highlights: A pleasant ride up the Slate Creek valley with a fairly easy grade and a pleasure on the return trip.

Land status: Bridger-Teton National Forest.

Maps: USGS Grizzly Lake, Mount Leidy.

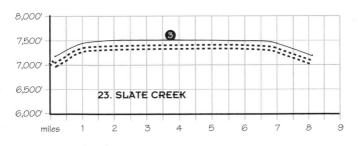

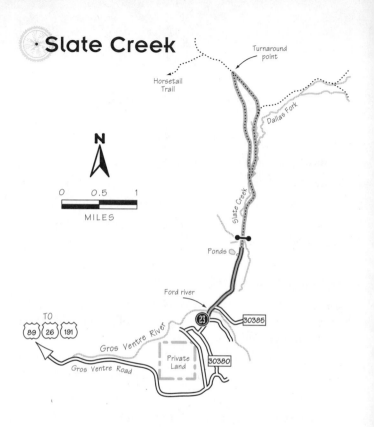

Slate Creek

Turnaround point

Horsetail Trail

Dallas Fork

N

0   0.5   1
MILES

Slate Creek

Ponds

Ford river

TO
89 26 191

30385

Gros Ventre River

Private Land

30380

Gros Ventre Road

Access: From Jackson, go north on U.S. Highway 26-89-191 for 7 miles. At Gros Ventre Junction, turn right (east) on Gros Ventre Road. Continue down road for 20 miles to the Crystal Creek Campground and continue for one more mile. Turn left (north) on Forest Road 30380 and follow road until it ends at the ROAD CLOSED sign at the Gros Ventre River.

Options: Other route options are to continue up the trail and connect with Horsetail Creek Trail or Ditch Creek.

Another option is to take the right fork at mile 3.4 and follow the Dallas Fork on a loop that returns to the trailhead.

The ride

0.0 Start at Road Closed sign. Go around gate and wade across the river.

0.1 Follow trail up the hill.

0.3 Reach summit of hill.

1.2 Pass small ponds.

1.4 Cross small creek. Old bridge has been washed out but culverts are still present.

1.5 Go through gate.

1.6 Wade across creek.

2.3 Cross creek.

3.1 Cross creek.

3.3 Bike hike through mud bog. Trail can be difficult to follow but just continue north.

3.4 Trail comes to a **T**. Go left. Right follows the Dallas Fork.

4.1 At fork in trail and turnaround point. Go around meadow on west side and then join the trail that goes down Slate Creek.

8.2 Back at start.

Horsetail Creek Out-and-Back

Location: Gros Ventre River Valley.

Distance: 6.6 miles.

Time: 2 to 3 hours.

Tread: ATV trail and singletrack.

Season: Best in the summer following spring runoff.

Aerobic level: Strenuous.

Technical difficulty: 3

Hazards: Steep and rocky areas.

Highlights: A strenuous climb up a creek drainage and a fast return on the way back down.

Land status: Bridger-Teton National Forest.

Maps: USGS Mount Leidy.

Access: From Jackson, go north on U.S. Highway 26-89-191 for 7 miles. At Gros Ventre Junction, turn right (east)

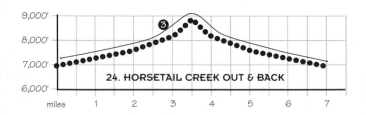

24. HORSETAIL CREEK OUT & BACK

Horsetail Creek Out-and-Back

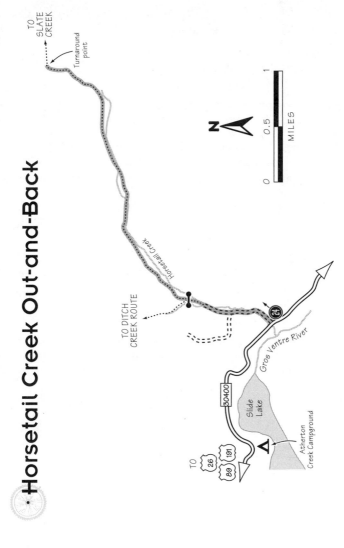

on Gros Ventre Road. Continue down road for 15.8 miles to Horsetail Creek trailhead.

Options: Other options are to connect with the Slate Creek Trail or the Ditch Creek Trail.

The ride

0.0 Begin at trailhead. Follow ATV trail north.
0.2 Cross creek.
0.6 Trail forks; go straight on singletrack (don't cross the creek).
0.7 Cross creek on rock-hop crossing.
0.9 Pass through gate. Trail forks immediately after; continue straight.
1.6 Cross creek.
1.8 Cross creek and then take steep uphill. Continue straight at top of hill.
2.1 Cross creek.
2.7 Enter a clearing. Trail gets steeper after clearing.
3.3 End of motorized trail with a spectacular view of the Teton Mountains. Turnaround point. Return on same route.
6.6 Back at trailhead.

Shadow Mountain

Shadow Mountain is popular with both mountain bikers and horseback riders. It rises along the eastern border of Antelope Flats. Most of the mountain is within Bridger-Teton National Forest, but the northwest corner is in Grand Teton National Park. The mountain lies in the shadow of the Tetons, whose stark craggy peaks rise to the west across the flat grassland of Antelope Flats.

There is dispersed camping on Shadow Mountain with a main undeveloped camping area at the base of the mountain. All routes described here start at the small parking area next to the forest service sign at the base of the mountain.

Shadow Mountain Loop

Location: Immediately east of Grand Teton National Park, approximately 10 miles northeast of Moose.

Distance: 9-mile loop.

Time: 2 to 3 hours.

Tread: Gravel road and doubletrack.

Season: Best from late spring through fall.

Aerobic level: Moderate.

Technical difficulty: 2

Hazards: Steep, rocky, and rutted section of gravel road; muddy potholes and ruts on the doubletrack.

Highlights: Views of the Tetons' craggy peaks.

Land status: Bridger-Teton National Forest, Grand Teton National Park.

Maps: USGS Moose, Shadow Mountain.

Access: From Jackson, go north on U.S. Highway 26-89-191 into Grand Teton National Park. A little over a mile past the Moose intersection, turn right onto Antelope Flats Road. Continue straight for 3 miles to a 4-way intersection.

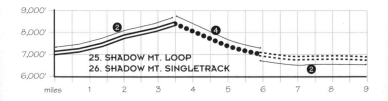

Shadow Mountain Loop

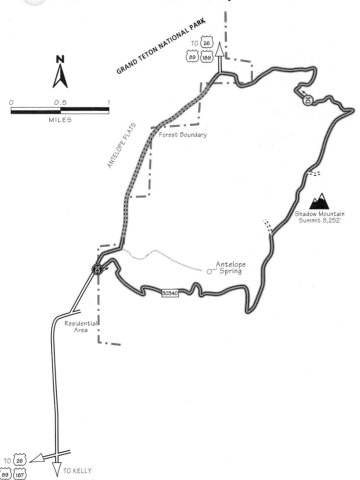

GRAND TETON NATIONAL PARK

TO 26
89 189

N

0   0.5   1
MILES

ANTELOPE FLATS

Forest Boundary

25

Shadow Mountain
Summit 8,252'

25

Antelope
Spring

30340

Residential
Area

TO 26
89 187

TO KELLY

Turn left onto the forest access road. After about 1.5 miles, the road enters national forest. Park near forest sign in one of the dispersed camping areas.

Options: Start ride at the 4-way intersection (park your car somewhere near this intersection). This adds 1.6 miles to the ride. Another alternative is to park at the same site as the Antelope Flats Loop (Ride 30). This adds 6.6 miles to the ride.

A singletrack trail forks west from the summit of Shadow Mountain and winds through the forest for a more challenging ride to the base of the mountain.

Additional doubletrack and hiking trails are worth exploring on Shadow Mountain and in the Gros Ventre Mountains to the east.

The ride

0.0 From parking area, go to the southeast on Forest Road 30340.

0.2 Begin steep uphill.

3.3 At summit.

3.7 Road forks. Stay left. Road becomes rougher and winds through pine and aspen woods.

5.6 Road forks. Go left.

6.2 Exit national forest and enter Grand Teton National Park.

6.6 Road forks. Go left onto rougher doubletrack and past buck-rail gate/fence. Right returns to highway.

8.8 Go past buck-rail fence.

9.0 Back at starting point.

Shadow Mountain Singletrack

Location: On Shadow Mountain, east of Grand Teton National Park.

Distance: 8.9-mile loop.

Time: 1.5 to 2.5 hours.

Tread: Gravel road, singletrack, and doubletrack.

Season: From late spring through fall.

Aerobic level: Strenuous.

Technical difficulty: 2+ on gravel road and doubletrack and 4 on singletrack.

Hazards: A few steep, rocky areas on gravel road; rock and log hazards on singletrack, which in some areas is similar to a bobsled run.

Highlights: Heart-thumping grind up Shadow Mountain; fun singletrack down the Shadow Mountain; view of the Tetons toward the west.

Land status: Bridger-Teton National Forest.

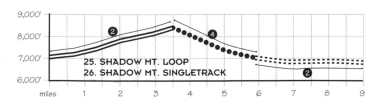

Shadow Mountain/ Antelope Spring

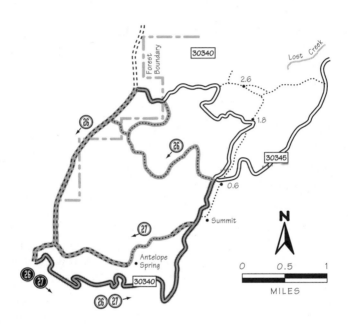

Maps: USGS Shadow Mountain.

Access: From Jackson, go north on U.S Highway 26-89-191 into Grand Teton National Park. A little over a mile past the Moose intersection, turn right onto Antelope Flats Road. Continue straight for 3 miles to a 4-way intersection. Turn left onto forest access road. After about 1.5 miles, the road enters Bridger-Teton National Forest. Park near forest sign in the dispersed camping area.

The ride

0.0 From parking area, go southeast on gravel Forest Road 30340.

0.2 Begin steep uphill.

3.3 At summit. Continue down gravel road.

3.7 Road forks. Stay left. Just past intersection, take singletrack trail that forks left. Trail forks several times between here and the bottom of the mountain. Stay left each time or explore other routes. All are singletrack trails that come out at the bottom of the mountain.

5.8 Turn left on doubletrack that follows along base of mountain.

8.9 Back at starting point.

Antelope Spring Loop

See map on page 110.

Location: On Shadow Mountain, east of Grand Teton National Park.

Distance: 5.6 miles.

Time: 1.5 to 2.5 hours.

Tread: Gravel road, doubletrack, and singletrack.

Season: From late spring through fall.

Aerobic level: Strenuous.

Technical difficulty: 2+ to 3.

Hazards: Steep, rocky areas with ruts on the gravel road; rock and log hazards on the way down.

Highlights: Heart-thumping grind up Shadow Mountain; fun singletrack down the Shadow Mountain; view of the Tetons toward the west.

Land status: Bridger-Teton National Forest.

Maps: USGS Shadow Mountain.

Access: From Jackson, go north on U.S Highway 26-89-191 into Grand Teton National Park. A little over a mile past the Moose intersection, turn right onto Antelope Flats Road. Continue straight for 3 miles to a 4-way intersection. Turn left onto the forest access road. After about 1.5 miles, the road enters national forest. Park near forest sign in one of the dispersed camping areas.

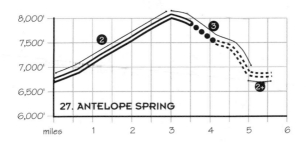

27. ANTELOPE SPRING

The ride

0.0 From parking area, go southeast on gravel Forest Road 30340.

0.2 Begin steep uphill.

3.3 Just before summit, doubletrack forks off left and goes south as it heads up the hill.

3.6 Pass through dispersed camping site onto singletrack trail. Begin downhill ride.

4.2 Trail turns to doubletrack.

4.5 Steep downhill goes off ridgeline and into drainage bottom.

4.6 Take right fork. Left goes up to Antelope Spring.

4.9 Come into clearing near bottom of mountain.

5.2 Trail joins main dirt road. Follow dirt road left (south).

5.6 Back at parking area.

Lost Creek Loop

Location: Shadow Mountain, immediately east of Grand Teton National Park.

Distance: 9.2 miles.

Time: 3 to 4 hours.

Tread: Everything from gravel to doubletrack to single-track.

Season: From late spring through fall.

Aerobic level: Strenuous.

Technical difficulty: 2+ to 3+.

Hazards: Rough and rocky sections of doubletrack and singletrack; potential for puddles on gravel road after heavy rain.

Highlights: Riding along Lost Creek; opportunities to explore old logging roads.

Land status: Bridger-Teton National Forest.

Maps: USGS Shadow Mountain.

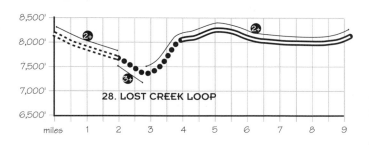

· Lost Creek Loop

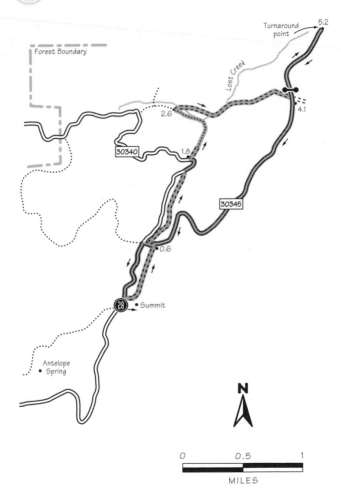

Turnaround point

5.2

Forest Boundary

Lost Creek

2.6

4.1

30340

1.8

30345

• 0.6

28 • Summit

Antelope
• Spring

N

| 0 | 0.5 | 1 |

MILES

Access: From Jackson, go north on U.S Highway 26-89-191 into Grand Teton National Park. A little over a mile past the Moose intersection, turn right onto Antelope Flats Road. Continue straight for 3 miles to a 4-way intersection. Turn left onto forest access road. After about 1.5 miles, the road enters national forest. Go southeast on Forest Road 30340 and up the mountain. After 3.6 miles, park vehicle in dispersed camping area.

The ride

0.0 Road forks, stay right (east).

0.1 Doubletrack splits. Go right on less traveled double-track. Stay right for 100 feet when road forks again.

0.6 Come to main gravel road, go left and follow road for 50 feet. Turn right onto doubletrack.

1.6 Come out on main road, passing by LODGEPOLE PINE TEST AREA sign. Go right on main road.

1.8 After curve, go past singletrack on right. This is an alternate route but it is very rocky. It's better to continue another 50 feet and turn right on old logging road.

1.9 Trail turns to singletrack.

2.6 Come out on doubletrack. Turn right. Left returns to main gravel road (FR 30345). After 50 feet, continue straight when trail forks.

2.8 Go through gate.

2.9 Cross creek.

3.1 Cross creek again.

4.1 Come to gravel road and go left on main Forest Road 30345. After 100 feet, pass by gate and continue straight.

4.5 Road forks; stay left.

4.6 Come to old clearcut. Stay on main road. Numerous

old logging roads branch off main road.

5.2 Road ends with great view looking north toward Yellowstone. Turn around and return back down road.

6.5 Back at gate. Continue straight on Forest Road 30345.

8.6 Come to intersection with Forest Road 30340. Go left up the hill.

9.2 Back at starting point.

Ditch Creek
Out-and-Back

Location: Shadow Mountain area, east of the Teton Science Camp.

Distance: 9.5 miles.

Time: 2 to 3 hours.

Tread: Doubletrack and singletrack.

Season: Best in summer following spring runoff.

Aerobic level: Moderate to strenuous.

Technical difficulty: 2+ to 3.

Hazards: The singletrack has some rocky areas but the rest of the trail is easy and smooth.

Highlights: A gentle climb up an old roadbed; technical singletrack with some easier sections.

Land status: Bridger-Teton National Forest.

Maps: USGS Shadow Mountain.

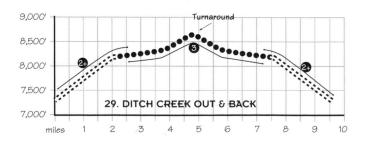

29. DITCH CREEK OUT & BACK

Ditch Creek

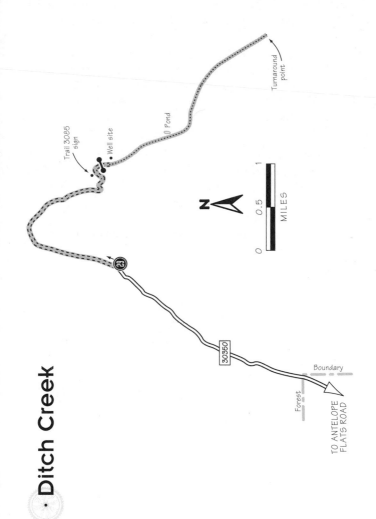

Trail 3085 sign

• Well site

Ø Pond

Turnaround point

N

0   0.5   1

MILES

30350

Forest

Boundary

TO ANTELOPE
FLATS ROAD

Access: From Jackson, go north on U.S. Highway 26-89-191 for 7 miles. At Gros Ventre Junction, turn right (east) on Gros Ventre Road. Continue down road through Kelly. At junction with Antelope Flats Road, continue straight on Antelope Flats Road. After a mile, turn right (east) on Forest Road 30350. Continue down road to Teton Science Camp. Go past the Science Camp and into the national forest. Continue down Forest Road 30350 until it ends at ROAD CLOSED sign. Route starts here.

Options: Alternate starting points include the junction of Antelope Flats and the Teton Science Camp road. There is a small parking area at the intersection. Other options are to start at the National Forest Boundary or at any point along Forest Road 30350.

You could continue down the trail instead of stopping at the turnaround point. The route eventually connects with Horsetail Creek.

The ride

0.0 Begin at end of road. Continue north on dirt road.
2.1 Pass by trail sign that says DITCH CREEK TRAIL #3085.
2.2 Go around gate.
2.7 Pass by old well pad site that has been revegetated. Trail becomes singletrack.
3.3 Pass through meadow area.
3.6 Pass by small pond.
4.9 Turnaround point is in open meadow. Trail drops down shortly past this point. Return on same route.
6.7 Pass by old well pad.
7.2 Back at gate.
9.5 Back at start.

Grand Teton

Both Grand Teton and Yellowstone National Parks are restrictive toward bicycles. Off-road travel is not allowed and bikes are not allowed on hiking trails. However, there are a few old roads closed to motorized travel that remain open to bicycles. Check with the rangers at the parks entrances to find additional biking opportunities.

Two rides are described in this section and both are easy rides that are great for sight-seeing.

Antelope Flats

Location: Grand Teton National Park.

Distance: 13.6-mile loop.

Time: 1.5 to 2.5 hours.

Tread: Paved road, doubletrack.

Season: Best from late spring through fall.

Aerobic level: Easy.

Technical difficulty: 1+ on paved road, 2+ on doubletrack.

Hazards: Rough pavement; traffic, especially on U.S. Highway 26-89-191; ruts in doubletrack and a washed-out section that must be bike hiked; bison near Blacktail Butte.

Highlights: This is a sight-seeing ride; great views of Grand Teton, Mount Moran, and the other peaks that make up the Tetons.

Land status: Grand Teton National Park.

Maps: USGS Moose, Shadow Mountain.

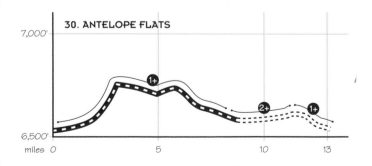

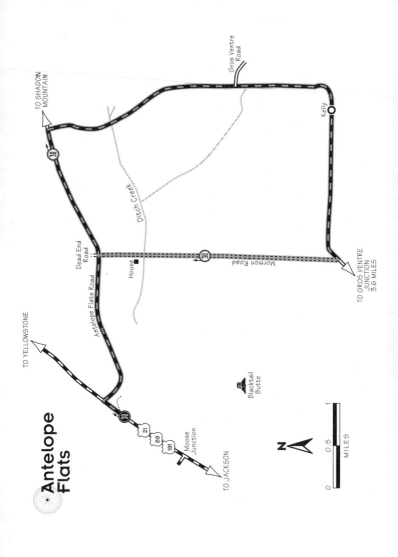

Antelope Flats

TO SHADOW MOUNTAIN

TO YELLOWSTONE

Gros Ventre Road

Kelly

Antelope Flats Road

Dead End Road

House

Ditch Creek

Mormon Road

TO GROS VENTRE JUNCTION 3.6 MILES

Blacktail Butte

Moose Junction

TO JACKSON

N

MILES
0   0.5   1

Access: From Jackson, go north on US 26-89-191 into Grand Teton National Park. One mile past the Moose intersection, park in the small parking area on the right side of the highway. This parking area is popular with local climbers going up a rock face on Blacktail Butte.

The ride

0.0 From parking area, go north on US 26-89-191. Be cautious of heavy traffic.

0.3 At Antelope Flats Road, turn right onto rough pavement.

2.1 Pass by Mormon Road. This will be the return route.

3.3 At four-way intersection. Go right. Left goes to Shadow Mountain.

4.9 Paved road goes left to Teton Science Camp. Continue straight.

5.8 Gros Ventre Road goes left. Continue straight to Kelly.

7.0 At Kelly. Turn left if you want to go into the little town. Continue straight and past a small store next to the road.

8.8 Turn right onto gravel Mormon Road. Straight goes past the Gros Ventre Campground.

8.9 Gravel road becomes rougher doubletrack. A sign may still be present that states the road is closed ahead. Don't worry, it is still passable to bicyclists.

9.9 Doubletrack goes right. Stay straight.

11.0 Come to ROAD CLOSED sign. Continue around it.

11.1 Walk across area where road is damaged.

11.2 Pass by residential home on the left.

11.5 Rejoin paved road. Turn left and return to starting point.

13.6 Back at starting area.

RKO Road Loop

Location: Grand Teton National Park.

Distance: 35.5 miles from Moose or 27.5 miles from Cottonwood Creek.

Time: 5 to 7 hours.

Tread: Paved road and dirt road.

Season: From late spring through fall.

Aerobic level: Easy.

Technical difficulty: 2+

Hazards: Obnoxiously rough and rutted sections on the RKO road; the paved road has been chipsealed and can be rough; watch for traffic.

Highlights: Very scenic ride that follows the Snake River via the RKO road.

Land status: Grand Teton National Park.

Maps: USGS Moose.

Access: From Jackson, go north on U.S. Highway 26-89-191 approximately 12 miles to Moose Junction. Turn

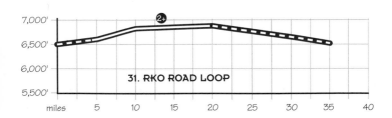

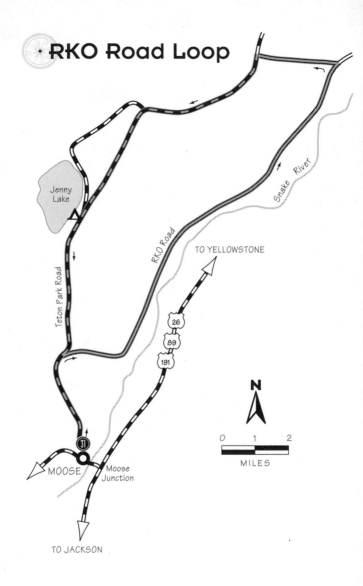

RKO Road Loop

Jenny Lake

Teton Park Road

RKO Road

Snake River

TO YELLOWSTONE

26
89
191

N

0   1   2
MILES

31
MOOSE   Moose
Junction

TO JACKSON

left (west) at the junction and continue to Moose. Route starts here or you can continue 4 more miles along Teton Park Road to Cottonwood Creek picnic area (for a 27.5-mile loop).

The ride

0.0 From Moose, go west on Teton Park Road.
4.0 Pass by Cottonwood Creek picnic area. Cross creek. Turn right (east) onto the RKO road, which is the first road on the east side of the pavement.
5.5 Road forks; go left.
11.1 Steep downhill segment.
13.0 Bear right at fork.
16.0 Road forks; stay left.
17.4 Turn left downhill.
19.5 Come to paved Teton Park Road. Turn left.
28.0 Jenny Lake Campground is on the right.
31.5 Back at Cottonwood Creek. Continue back on road to Moose.
35.5 Back at beginning.

Appendix A

National Forest Service Offices

Bridger-Teton National Forest
P.O. Box 1888
Jackson, WY 83001
(307) 739–5500

Jackson Ranger District
P.O. Box 1689
Jackson, WY 83001
(307) 739–5400

Big Piney Ranger District
Highway 189
P.O. Box 218
Big Piney, WY 83113
(307) 276–3375

Buffalo Ranger District
P.O. Box 278
Moran, WY 83013
(307) 543–2386

Greys River Ranger District
125 Washington
P.O. Box 338
Afton, WY 83110
(307) 886–3166

Pinedale Ranger District
P.O. Box 220
Pinedale, WY 82941
(307) 367–4326

Grand Teton National Park
P.O. Drawer 170
Moose, WY 83012
(307) 739–3300
(307) 739–3399
Visitor Information

Appendix B

Index of Rides

Glossary of Mountain Biking Terms

ATB: All-terrain bicycle; a.k.a. mountain bike, sprocket rocket, fat tire flyer.

ATV: All-terrain vehicle; in this book ATV refers to motorbikes and three- and four-wheelers designed for off-road use.

Bail: Getting off the bike, usually in a hurry, and whether or not you meant to. Often a last resort.

Bunny hop: Leaping up, while riding, and lifting both wheels off the ground to jump over an obstacle (or for sheer joy).

Clamper cramps: That burning, cramping sensation experienced in the hands during extended braking.

Clean: To ride without touching a foot (or other body part) to the ground; to ride a tough section successfully.

Clipless: A type of pedal with a binding that accepts a special cleat on the soles of bike shoes. The cleat clicks in for more control and efficient pedaling and out for safe landings (in theory).

Contour: A line on a topographic map showing a continuous elevation level over uneven ground. Also used as a verb to indicate a fairly easy or moderate grade: "The trail contours around the canyon rim before the final grunt to the top."

Dab: To put a foot or hand down (or hold onto or lean on a tree or other support) while riding. If you have to dab, then you haven't ridden that piece of trail **clean.**

Downfall: Trees that have fallen across the trail.

Doubletrack: A trail, Jeep road, ATV route, or other track with two distinct ribbons of **tread,** typically with grass growing in between. No matter which side you choose, the other rut always looks smoother.

Endo: Lifting the rear wheel off the ground and riding (or abruptly not riding) on the front wheel only. Also known, at various degrees of control and finality, as a nose wheelie, "going over the handlebars," and a face plant.

Fall line: The angle and direction of a slope; the **line** you follow when gravity is in control and you aren't.

Graded: When a gravel road is scraped level to smooth out the washboards and potholes, it has been graded. In this book, a road is listed as graded only if it is regularly maintained. Not all such roads are graded every year, however.

Granny gear: The lowest (easiest) gear, a combination of the smallest of the three chainrings on the bottom bracket spindle (where the pedals and crank arms attach to the bike's frame) and the largest cog on the rear cluster. Shift down to your granny gear for serious climbing.

Hammer: To ride hard; derived from how it feels afterward: "I'm hammered."

Hammerhead: Someone who actually enjoys feeling **hammered.** A Type-A personality rider who goes hard and fast all the time.

Kelly hump: An abrupt mound of dirt across the road or trail. These are common on old logging roads and skidder tracks, placed there to block vehicle access. At high speeds, they become launching pads for bikes and inadvertent astronauts.

Line: The route (or trajectory) between or over obstacles or through turns. **Tread** or trail refers to the ground you're riding on; the line is the path you choose within the tread (and exists mostly in the eye of the beholder).

Off-the-seat: Moving your butt behind the bike seat and over the rear tire; used for control on extremely steep descents. This position increases braking power, helps prevent **endos,** and reduces skidding.

Portage: To carry the bike, usually up a steep hill, across unrideable obstacles, or through a stream.

Quads: Thigh muscles (short for quadriceps) or maps in the USGS topographic series (short for quadrangles). Nice quads of either kind can help get you out of trouble in the backcountry.

Ratcheting: Also known as backpedaling; pedaling backward to avoid hitting rocks or other obstacles with the pedals.

Sidehill: Where the trail crosses a slope. If the **tread** is narrow, keep your inside (uphill) pedal up to avoid hitting the ground. If the tread tilts downhill, you may have to use some body language to keep the bike plumb, or vertical, to avoid slipping out.

Singletrack: A trail, game run, or other track with only one ribbon of **tread.** Good singletrack is pure fun.

Spur: A side road or trail that splits off from the main route.

Surf: Riding through loose gravel or sand, when the wheels sway from side to side. Also *heavy surf:* frequent and difficult obstacles.

Suspension: A bike with front suspension has a shock-absorbing fork or stem. Rear suspension absorbs shock between the rear wheel and frame. A bike with both is said to be fully suspended.

Switchbacks: When a trail goes up a steep slope, it *zigzags* or *switchbacks* across the **fall line** to ease the gradient of the climb. Well-designed switchbacks make a turn with at least an 8-foot radius and remain fairly level within the turn itself. These are rare, however, and cyclists often struggle to ride through sharply angled, sloping switchbacks.

Track stand: Balancing on a bike in one place, without rolling forward appreciably. Cock the front wheel to one side and bring that pedal up to the one or two o'clock position. Now control your side-to-side balance by applying pressure on the pedals and brakes and changing the angle of the front wheel, as needed. It takes practice but really comes in handy at stoplights, on **switchbacks,** and when trying to free a foot before falling.

Tread: The riding surface, particularly regarding **singletrack.**

Water bar: A log, rock, or other barrier placed in the **tread** to divert water off the trail and prevent erosion. Peeled logs can be slippery and cause bad falls, especially when they angle sharply across the trail.

Whoop-dee-doo: A series of kelly humps used to keep vehicles off trails. Watch your speed or do the dreaded top tube tango.

About the Author

Amber Travsky is a wildlife biologist, environmental consultant, karate instructor, freelance writer, mountain biker, and all-around outdoorswoman. She and her husband, Rich, reside in Laramie, where she served two terms as mayor and nine years on the City Council.

Amber currently chairs the Wyoming Governor's Council for Physical Fitness and Sport and is a member of the President's Council for Physical Fitness and Sport. She has earned the rank of 5th Degree Black Belt and owns the Laramie Kempo Karate Club. She also runs an environmental consulting company, Real West Natural Resource Consulting, and is the outdoor columnist for the *Wyoming Tribune-Eagle* in Cheyenne.

Help Us Keep This Guide Up to Date

Every effort has been made by the author and editors to make this guide as accurate and useful as possible. However, many things can change after a guide is published—establishments close, phone numbers change, hiking trails are rerouted, and so on.

We would love to hear from you concerning your experiences with this guide and how you feel it could be improved and kept up to date. While we may not be able to respond to all comments and suggestions, we'll take them to heart and we'll also make certain to share them with the author. Please send your comments and suggestions to the following address:

The Globe Pequot Press
Reader Response/Editorial Department
P.O. Box 480
Guilford, CT 06437

Or you may e-mail us at:

editorial@globe-pequot.com

Thanks for your input, and happy biking!